Letters of Long Ago

by Agnes Just Reid

Fourth edition edited by Douglass J. Reid and Rick Just

Letters of Long Ago

By Agnes Just Reid

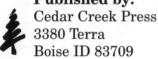

Published by:
Cedar Creek Press
3380 Terra
Boise ID 83709

Copyright © 1997 by Presto Preservation Association

Most of the proceeds from the sale of this book go to the Presto Preservation Association, Inc. This non-profit Idaho corporation is dedicated to preserving the history of Nels and Emma Just and their descendants. Projects include a bi-annual newsletter, pioneer cemetery preservation, and the restoration of the original Just home. For information, or to subscribe to the newsletter, write to the Presto Preservation Association, Inc., 3380 Terra, Boise ID 83709.

Publisher's Cataloging in Publication
(Prepared by Quality Books Inc.)

Reid, Agnes Just, 1886-1976
    Letters of long ago / Agnes Just Reid. -- [New ed.].
    p. cm.
    Reprint with additions of 1973 ed.
    ISBN 0-9653539-4-X

1. Reid, Agnes Just, 1886-1976 2. Idaho--History. 3. Frontier and pioneer life--Idaho 4. Morrisite War, 1862. I. Title.

F746.R35 1997   917.96'03'30924
                                              QBI96-40582

To my Mother

Whose life motto has been:

"Do unto your children as you wish your parents had done unto you."

This book is affectionately dedicated by

HER DAUGHTER

Contents

About the cover

The cover of this edition was designed by Rosemary Hardin of Acme Communications in Boise, Idaho.

The pastel of Nels and Emma Just's "big house" was done in the 1960s by Idaho Falls, Idaho artist Helen Aupperle. It hung for many years in Agnes Just Reid's home, and was one of her most prized possessions.

Aupperle was born Helen Hoff in Idaho Falls in 1905. Many of her pieces, including this one were signed Helen Hoff, even after her marriage to Don Aupperle.

She received a Bachelor of Arts degree from UCLA, a Masters of Art from Claremont College and also studied at the Royal Academy of Art in Sweden. Aupperle was a founder and charter member of Idaho Falls Art Guild, and the Idaho Art Guild. She taught art in Idaho Falls schools for 23 years and designed art classrooms at Skyline and Idaho Falls high schools. Helen Aupperle died in 1971.

Introduction

Family histories are precious to the families they describe. *Letters of Long Ago,* now in its fourth printing, is such a history, but it is so much more. The book is a classic tale of the West, skillfully told by a woman who was there for the early chapters.

It was a proud moment for the Just-Reid family when the University of Utah selected *Letters of Long Ago* to be a part of their series, "Utah, the Mormons, and the West" in 1973. For the first time in decades this cherished history was available again to every family member.

Then, decades slipped by again. Every last copy of the third edition of the book had been purchased, and the book was out of print. The family grew. Idaho grew dramatically, and the new residents were hungry for history of their home. It was time to bring back this time-honored chronicle of one woman's life in the West.

Cedar Creek Press, in cooperation with the Presto Preservation Association, is proud to present this special printing of *Letters of Long Ago.* The original story by Agnes Just Reid, as it appeared in the first edition, begins on page 1, following this introduction. You may wish to skip right to her work. It is poignant prose that needs no help from any present-day writer. The introduction, the epilogue and the footnotes provide background and a deeper look at some of the incidents described in the letters.

Most of the ancillary material was published in the University of Utah edition, edited by Dr. Brigham D. Madsen. We are indebted to his scholarly work. Additional and clarifying material was located by the family in the intervening years. For the first time, all is available in one edition.

Illustrations by Mabel Bennett Hutchinson

Mabel Bennett Hutchinson in 1993 with her watercolor of Nels and Emma Just's "big house."

This book brings back the charming chapter heading sketches by Mabel Bennett Hutchinson. Mabel is the daughter of Fred and Agnes Bennett, and granddaughter of Nels and Emma Just. As a teenage ranch girl, and close cousin of Agnes Just Reid, Mabel was thrilled to be asked to illustrate the original book. Agnes was her mentor. Mabel's drawings show the natural artistic ability that would one day, with some formal training and years of practice, blossom into a widely recognized talent. A well-known California watercolorist in the 40s and 50s, Mabel was renowned in the 1960's for wood collages, constructions and totems. Her art and papers, including the original sketches for *Letters of Long Ago*, were recently collected by the Smithsonian Institution to be preserved for the enjoyment of future generations. At this writing, Mabel Bennett Hutchinson is 93, and living at her home in Capistrano Beach, California. She has never ceased being an artist, frequently hand illustrating her correspondence. At 91, she began experimenting with abstract photographs.

Selected material from Dr. Brigham Madsen's introduction to the third edition

When *Letters of Long Ago* was first published by The Caxton Printers, Ltd., in 1923, oral history was not the accepted branch of historical art it is today. In fact, the first edition did not explain that the letters were written by Agnes Just Reid as she listened to her mother, Emma Thompson Just, relate incidents from her life as a pioneer on the Blackfoot River in Idaho during the 1870s and 80s.

To ensure the reader would understand the events depicted in the life of Emma Just were true and actual happenings, Agnes Just Reid included an Introduction in the second edition of 1936 which reads:

"The incidents and dates recorded in these letters are all absolutely true, but the letters themselves are fiction. My mother lived the letters, and I wrote them as the most plausible way of combining events of such varying character.

"Such correspondence did take place during the twenty-four years that my grandfather lived in England, but the letters were not preserved through the years.

"Each letter was censored by my mother as it came from the typewriter, but, because of the delay caused by two different periodicals starting to run them serially, my mother died while the first edition was on the press."

In preparation for the third edition of *Letters of Long Ago,* Dr. Everett L. Cooley, general editor of the University of Utah series in which the book was included, and Dr. Brigham D. Madsen undertook to record some oral history of their own by interviewing Agnes Just Reid in her home on the Blackfoot River. This was in September 1972 when Mrs. Reid was 86 and still writing a weekly column for the

Blackfoot News, an assignment which she started in 1935. In answer to Dr. Cooley's questions she explained further the process of oral history which she employed:

Dr. Cooley: *When you wrote this, was it written strictly from memory or did you have notes that you used as prompters?*

Mrs. Reid: *My mother was still here so if there was anything I doubted or needed setting straight on she was right here to ask and she had the best memory. She could recount things the way they happened.*

Dr. Cooley: *Did she actually read the manuscript as you wrote?*

Mrs. Reid: *Yes, everything she read as it came from the typewriter.*

Agnes Just Reid has given us a classic account of pioneer life in the form of letters so skillfully and artistically drawn that the reader is able to share the triumphs, frustrations, happinesses, and sorrows in the full life of Emma Just as she builds a home and rears a family in Blackfoot Valley.

Letters of Long Ago describes with remarkable insight and poignancy the experiences of a pioneer woman on the edge of an Indian reservation in southeastern Idaho where loneliness and hardship were commonplace. Agnes Just Reid captures the thoughts and innermost feelings of her mother with compassion and love in this moving and eloquent account of Emma Just's struggle to raise a family and build a home in a wilderness area.

A brief history of Emma's family

Emma's parents, George Thompson and Frances Hunter Thompson, joined the Mormon church in England and emigrated to America, then to Utah in 1853-54. Daughters Emma, almost four, and Georgianna, 15 months, began the trip with them, but the latter died December 19, 1853 "on the sea." A son, George William, was born to the couple, April 10, 1854 "in America," and died seven weeks later at St. Louis, Missouri, according to records made in George Thompson's handwriting. Although L.D.S. church records are quite complete concerning new converts traveling to the West, the church newspaper, the *Deseret News,* ran out of newsprint for the six months of the 1854 traveling season. Because of that, it was assumed there was no account of the Thompson family's migration when the Third Edition of *Letters of Long Ago* was published in 1973. A brief account of the trip, penned by Emma and dated 1903, was recently discovered among her personal papers. It is included here for the first time:

"We must have left England some time in the winter of '53. Reached Utah in Nov. '54.

"I was the only child at this time. We started to cross the plains some time early in '54. My father drove an ox team for an invalid who had a good outfit but was unable to drive. We started from Leavenworth, Kansas.

"I cannot remember much about it, only days and days in a covered wagon. . . once the whole train had to stop to let a big herd of buffalo pass. . . they were the only ones I ever saw. . . I can recall some painted Indians, two or three, sitting in the front of the wagon, asking for many things.

"The sick man told my mother to give them anything they wanted, if they would just go. After getting some few articles of food they left. . . The next circumstance is of a woman being killed. Fell out of the wagon one night when we were driving late. I distinctly remember seeing her lying in a tent. One ear was bloody.

"On arriving in Salt Lake the invalid, his team and all his belongings were given over to the Mormon elders he had seen in England. . . He died soon after. His only wish was to live long enough to see "Zion."

"My parents also belonged to the Mormons, joined in England. . . somehow we came to Ogden. . . our first house was a log room 10 x 12 which had been used as a chicken coop. It was large enough to hold all our possessions, but such a home. . . such a <u>Zion</u> as we had been told of.

"My mother was not a very strong believer, and Father's faith began to weaken as he realized the difference between seeing and hearing missionaries <u>tell</u> of the 'land flowing with milk and honey.' He soon became opposed to their ways, which did not improve our conditions among them in those early days."

A brief history of Nels' family

The PeterAnderson Just and Karen Marie Christensen Just family joined the Mormon church in Denmark and traveled to the New World in 1857. Accompanying them were their five sons, Christen, Nels, Jens, Joseph and Hyrum—the last two names indicative of the period when the Justs accepted the L.D.S. faith. Second son Nels, a central figure in this book, was 10 years old at the time.

The family left Liverpool, England, on April 25, 1857, aboard the ship *Westmoreland* which carried "544 souls," 540 from Scandinavia and four presiding elders from England, under the direction of Mathias Cowley. The ship crossed the Atlantic in 36 days and arrived at Philadelphia May 31, 1857. The group of immigrants then traveled by rail to Baltimore, Maryland, then to Wheeling, Virginia, finally arriving at Iowa City, Iowa, on June 9, 1857. From here they traveled by wagon to Florence, Nebraska, where two companies were formed: the Mathias Cowley Wagon Train and the Christian Christiansen Handcart Company. The Just family traveled with the Christiansen Handcart Company which was the seventh handcart company of Mormon Saints to cross the plains and the second and last in 1857. There were 330 "souls," 68 handcarts, three wagons, and 10 mules in the company. The Cowley Wagon Train left Florence on July 6, the Christiansen Handcart Company left on July 7, and the two arrived in Salt Lake City on the same day, September 13, 1857.

The Mormon families renounce their religion
Not much is known of the Just family from the time of their arrival in Utah to their removal to Soda Springs, Idaho, by 1863. The Thompsons apparently settled first in Ogden, Utah. But both families became caught up in the excitement of the Morrisite movement, left the Mormon church, and suffered the fate of most of the other Morrisites.

The story of the Morrisites
Joseph Morris, a convert to Mormonism from England, reached Utah in 1853 and by 1857 was beginning to report visions and meetings with Christ which soon alienated him from the main body of Mormons. He began to attract followers and was finally excommunicated when he announced some 300 revelations from Christ. In 1861 he established his own church, ordained 12 apostles, built Fort Kington on the south bank of Weber River where it flows into the Salt Lake Valley, and gathered his converts around him.

Within a year, the Morrisite church had 425 adherents and preached that the Second Coming of Christ was at hand. The group also became militant, denouncing Brigham Young, training and disciplining the male members into a small military force, and preparing to take over the Utah settlement, after which the entire United States was to be conquered preparatory to the establishment of the Kingdom of God on the whole earth.

The neighboring Mormon settlers became increasingly apprehensive at the war-like utterances and activities of the Morrisites, but the incident which led to the "Morrisite War" was the imprisonment of three dissident converts who tried to escape from Fort Kington. The wives of the three men finally appealed for help from the territorial authorities to free their husbands, and in response, a writ was issued, to be served by Robert T. Burton, deputy marshal.

A federal posse under Burton overpowered the Morrisites, killing several of their number and capturing the rest. Ninety Morrisites were arrested for resisting due process of law, 60 were tried by jury, and 10 were indicted by a grand jury for murder. Seven men were found guilty of murder and sentenced from 10 to 15 years imprisonment at hard labor. Those found guilty of impeding justice as served by the posse were fined $100 each. Three days after the court action, the territorial governor granted all of them a full pardon.

The beleaguered Morrisites now sought the protection of the troops at Camp Douglas and in May 1863, Captain David Black and a military escort accompanied a group of them to the Soda Springs area where they founded Morristown, named for their fallen leader. Both the Just and Thompson families moved to the Soda Springs area after the battle at Kington Fort.

A tragic side road in Emma's life

Nels Just and Emma Thompson were acquainted at Soda Springs, but Emma married one of the petty officers of the Connor command, George Bennett, while the families resided there. Emma was 15 at the time of her marriage in February 1865, and "thought she had won a prize" in her soldier husband. The couple moved to Salt Lake City and Camp Douglas for about 10 months. From there they moved back to Soda Springs in April 1866; to Lincoln Valley during the summer of 1866; to Taylor Bridge on the Snake River for the winter of 1866-67; to Ross Fork, not far from their Lincoln Valley residence in March, 1867, where they were in charge of the Wells-Fargo stage station for a few months; and finally, in July, 1867 to Montana.

Disillusioned with religion and uncomfortable in their life at Soda Springs, George Thompson decided in 1868 to return to England with his wife and infant daughter Kate, who had been born April 1, 1867. They visited Emma and George Bennett at Ross Fork and asked them to return to England with them. The Bennetts agreed to do so.

Traveling separately, the Thompsons by ox team and the Bennetts with a team of ponies, the two families were

to meet in late summer at Helena, Montana, and catch a
Missouri River steamboat for the journey downriver, and
eventually to an ocean port for the trip to England.
But George Bennett, who by this time could not "be
trusted as soon as he got where there was liquor," had
decided against the journey, though he had not confided
this to his wife.

Arriving at Helena some time before the Thompsons,
the Bennetts found a place to stay outside the town in a
miner's cabin. Emma, trusting her husband to connect up
with her parents when they arrived, seldom went into town.

Rather than seeking out the Thompsons, George
Bennett had avoided his in-laws so as also to avoid going
to England with them as planned.

The Thompsons camped for a week on Helena's main
street waiting for their daughter and her husband to join
them. As the last boat of the season prepared to leave, the
parents were forced to embark, leaving Emma behind to
wonder what had befallen them. Several bewildering and
worrisome months later, in early 1868, Emma got word
her mother had never reached home, but died September
28, 1867 in Liverpool. Emma's baby sister died two days
later in East Winch, the Thompson's family home.

The Bennetts remained in Helena for some months
following the Thompson's return to England, then moved
to Deer Lodge, where George was employed at a livery
stable, both as a bookkeeper and as a helper around the
horses.

By fall 1868 Emma was pregnant and George had added
gambling to his penchant for liquor. He had also robbed
his employer, stolen a horse from the stable and left town.

Deserted by her husband, Emma was befriended by a
Catholic couple at Deer Lodge. They took her into their
home, saw her through the birth of her son, Fred Bennett,
in March, 1869 and helped her secure a divorce.

Three weeks after the birth of his child, George Bennett,
having been apprehended and jailed for a time, visited
Emma and his first-born, begging forgiveness. His

mistreated wife refused to reconcile. He visited them once more, bringing some small gifts for his son. As far as is known, there was no further contact between George Bennett and Emma or his son.

The story of Nels and Emma begins

In the fall of 1869, Emma returned to the Blackfoot River to be with her uncle and aunt, Charles and Jane Higham. After a year of living with the Highams, she renewed her friendship with Nels Just. This book begins with their marriage.

The Wedding

Blackfoot River, Idaho Territory
December 2, 1870

My Dear Father:

I am not sure you will approve of the step I have taken, but I hope you will. I was married on the ninth of last month to a young man I had become acquainted with at the home of my aunt. Perhaps it was not the sensible thing to do, but you see, since my divorce two years ago I have been just sort of drifting. I left good friends and good opportunities in Montana to come here to my nearest of kin, thinking I would be more contented, but I found the work with my aunt very hard and the conditions, in general, harder than the work. You disapproved of my going on the stage, and after the baby came I was thankful that you had. For babies cry for a home with the first breath they draw. So my baby, who is becoming quite a lad, is to have a home, built by a stepfather, but a home for all of that.

We had a queer wedding journey. I wish some of your friends there in that great city of London might have seen us and smiled, I was sitting in the covered wagon with my little boy, while the prospective bridegroom trudged along in the dust and sand trying to get two yoke of oxen over the ground fast enough to reach a justice of the peace before we were overtaken by winter. They are not record-breaking cattle, but they are as good as any in the valley, even though they did consume eight days in making the trip to Malad.[1]

The journey was not unpleasant, for the weather was fine, as you well know, it usually is here in the fall. At night the air would be crisp and cool, but my good comrade tied the cover down tightly over the wagon, so my boy and I were safe and snug while he stood guard over us. The country is full of wolves and Indians, but neither seem at all hostile toward us. As you know, the greatest fear the traveler entertains is that his oxen may stray away.

That reminds me that I have not told you why we are starting our new home on the Blackfoot River. Nels has been doing some freighting during the time I had known him and once when the cattle slipped away from him during the night, they came to this very spot. The stage road is about six miles from here, so he soon followed them and found a wonderful little valley divided from the Snake River Valley by a strip of bench land and not visible from the stage line.[2]

From that day he has carried a vision with him, a vision of the home that we are founding today. Oh, father, it is a bleak looking place to think of spending one's life in, but we have pure water, fresh air, fish and game in abundance, and room, room, any amount of it.

Our capital in stock was $125, and it took most of it to buy a cook stove and lumber for a floor in the cabin that is to be. We brought up some freight for Uncle and received in payment a small amount of flour, but I think enough to last through the winter. And we have, my dear father, your parting gift to me, three cows. Uncle kept the increase for the trouble they had been to him, but we have the cows and are truly grateful to you. Don't worry about us. We are both young and both able and willing to work, so that perseverance is all we need. Besides, this is luxury compared with the hard times in Utah some years back. We all came through even that, and you were always cheerful, giving your shares to mother and to us children and going without yourself.

Poor Mother, how she must have suffered! She could not stand the way of the West, for she had been accustomed to comforts. With me it is different, I have no recollection of anything but privation, and as long as I can see the sun rise I am going to have courage, but oh, do not ask me to come to you. That dreadful, sickening stretch of water lies between us, and that dreadful London fog will be there to greet me, so I cannot come. How I wish you had stayed with me, since Mother was never permitted to reach her beloved England anyway, but we might have blamed ourselves if you had not made the effort.

There are times, though, when I need you so. I need your hopeful philosophy, your chronic content. I shall grow old gladly if I can, but hope to attain some measure of your contentment. Don't worry about me, Father, there will be no drunkenness in this marriage, and therefore no divorce. Sometimes I feel uneasy because of my lack of real, all forgiving love that guided my other marriage, but again I wonder what that great love gave me but misery. There is no deception, for my husband knows that I do not care as I should, but he, foolish boy, thinks that he cares enough for both of us. I call him a boy, though he is two years older, but he looks so very youthful. And a marriage, a divorce and a son make me feel very ancient.

I wish I could put on paper some of the youngster's attempts at conversation. It would do your heart good. He calls his stepfather "Nee," the best he can do for Nels. Anyway, you can rest assured that he is a good healthy, normal youngster. Whatever frailties were brought from the old country to shorten the lives of your children ha been weeded out in this generation.

With our best love,
Your Emma

*Emma
Thompson
Bennett, age 16.*

The House Beautiful

Blackfoot River, Idaho Territory
April 11, 1871

My dear Father:

Our first winter has been a very pleasant one. Very little snow and an early "breaking up." I rather feared a winter like the one we spent in Soda Springs and had that been the case I could not have had your letter for several weeks yet, as we have to go twenty miles for even the possibility of a letter and it often ends in just a possibility, for the service is very uncertain. The mail is carried by the stage drivers and left at the station that seems most convenient.

How glad I am that you remember Nels from old Soda Springs days, and were favorably impressed by his worthiness. I did not mention the fact that he had lived there, thinking that you, like myself, would be unable to remember him. Oh, there was nothing for us girls to see and remember those days but blue coats and brass buttons! Why at the mature age of 15, when I married my soldier boy, I regarded a half-grown Danish lad as quite beneath my notice.

Yet, that is what my husband of today was then, and the worst of it is that he remembers me perfectly in all my complacency.

Our first "house" is not one that would be likely to lure Queen Victoria from her throne, but it is ours, because we have made it with the simple materials that God left strewn around here for us. It is only a hole in the ground, it differs from the habitations of the lesser animals, however, in the flatness of its walls and the squareness of its corners. It has no windows, but is lighted by a tallow dip and the cheerful fire on the hearth. We feel very wealthy because of our cook stove. You and I, Father, lived and laughed in the days of the open fire. So with the stove to furnish us heat and a splendid heavy buffalo skin to keep the cold from coming in the opening that we use for a door, we have kept comfortable.

For furniture, well, first we have a wonderful bedstead that Nels has made. Four legs made from a pine pole, with holes bored in them to put in side pieces, which are also made of pine poles. Then down the sides are many holes bored and through them run strips of cowhide, laced back and forth, making springs. For mattress we have a tick filled with cured bunchgrass, that was cut with a scythe while the weather was warm. We have one chair, only one that I brought with me from Montana, and a table of rough pine boards that was given to us by a man at Fort Hall. We each had bedding and our dishes are so few I hate to enumerate.

Things will be better, though, even in another year, for we have many plans for building and improving, but there is no work that will bring in anything. Last year it was different, there was work for everyone while they were building the fort eleven miles from here. Aunt and I made good money. I baked bread for thirty-five men, which meant thirty-five loaves, in a little number seven stove. That alone was quite a day's work, but they paid me either five cents a loaf or pound for pound of flour. That is, when I used a pound of flour for soldier bread I put a pound aside for ourselves and in the course of the summer it grew into a mighty pile. Besides this, Aunt and I together cooked for six of the mechanics, milked twenty cows and sold butter and milk to the soldiers, did washing and anything that would bring in money. I used to be dreadfully tired, but it was not so bad, and how I wish now that we had some of the work and some of the pay, it would help so much in the building of another house.[3]

We take the *New York Sun* and *Peterson's Magazine*. The stories of Frances Hodgson are running in the magazine and I like them so much.[4] Mr. Shoemaker is also very kind to loan us reading matter and he has a better supply than anyone. They live a little more than two miles down the river, but she is in such poor health that she seldom gets out of the house. Speaking of reading, I must tell you that Nels and I had one of our first quarrels over Shakespeare. He has his complete works in the cheapest edition obtainable and he reads and reads until sometimes he forgets to carry a bucket of water. Well, I felt very much abused and told him so. I know now that I was wicked, for I should be glad that he can be entertained in that manner. I've seen all of his best plays again and again, but I will not give my poor husband time to even read them. Women are surely funny folks.

We shall plant a small garden, very small though, for the problem of irrigation is the next one. We have the land and we have the water, but the next thing is to bring them together. This year the garden will be a hand-made affair, watered with a bucket.

The spring has brought some activities of the kind

peculiar to frontier localities. An occasional trapper drops in on his way to a summer job or to market the furs from his winter's catch. How we welcome such company! Some of these fellows have good educations and have drifted here from the states, where everything is civilized. We listen to them eagerly, beg them to remain longer to share our primitive hospitalities and sigh when they pass on.

Freddie sends you a big hug and wishes you would come and see us. I join in the wish, but I know that you will enjoy being quiet for a few years after the travel and hardship of the past.

With my best love,
Emma

Nels Just, age 35.

A Son is Born

Blackfoot River, Idaho Territory
November 15, 1871

My Dear Father:

Another little grandson for you before you have ever seen the first one. Born October 26th to a most disappointed mother. I did so want him to be a girl. I guess everyone wants the first born to be a son but after that surely one should be allowed "a little sister." So I had my plans all laid that way, without giving a thought to his father's interest in the matter, and poor little rascal, I hardly forgave him until he was three days old. Then his father said very gallantly, and I knew truthfully, as well, that he had always wanted him to be a boy, so I suppose the poor little chap will feel at least half welcome. His coming was a marvel, and still is. I confess I had dreaded it, with a dread that every mother must feel in repeating the experience of childbearing. I could only think that another birth would mean another pitiful struggle of days' duration, followed by months of weakness, as it had been before. Then at the eleventh hour my Aunt refused to be with me because of some little differences Nels had had with her two boys. The world did not look very bright just at that point in our history. However, my good Nettie offered to leave her husband to do his own housekeeping to help us, and three days after she came little Jimmie was born. Born with so little travail that I scarcely had time to know I was in labor until I heard his cry. Then Nettie, dear tender-hearted Nettie, our only help, broke down and could not do a thing for either of us. So Nels was our surgeon and I my own nurse. They brought me the clothes and the water and I washed and dressed my own child just as a Bannock squaw would have done. In fact, I think I am going back to them. I feel each day that I am becoming less and less civilized and more and more a part of the wild waste around me. I have lived in the open much during the summer, riding and driving a great deal. Why, only a little more than a month before my confinement, Nels and I went fishing up the river on horseback and on the way home I was a little behind and as Nels rounded a bend in the river and went out of sight, my horse became frightened and ran to overtake him. I was carrying my fish pole and it frightened me so I did not ride any more.

When baby was three days old Nettie had to go home so I got up and helped with the work, then when he was only ten, Nels had to go for our winter supplies so that left me with the milking, just one cow now, and wood carrying. I guess I rather overdid the thing, for I took quite sick during his absence and I don't know just how I could have managed, but "Old Wood," one of our bachelor friends, happened in and found me, so he came regularly after that until Nels got back.

I must not forget to tell you that we have a new house, a cabin twelve by fourteen, and all of our costly (?) furnishings from the dugout are moved into it. Nels worked several days for a man at the stage station at $1.50 per day, and immediately paid a neighbor who lives less than a mile up the river, the same amount to help him build the cabin.[5] We have sold the two yoke of oxen, too, and have a pony team. The oxen brought four hundred dollars.

During the early spring Nels had a very small contract for a very small irrigating system. He brought water from Willow Creek, a distance of two miles, to Eagle Rock, where the Andersons have a store and toll bridge.[6] He did it all with a shovel and a good deal in the spirit of a joke, still they paid him one hundred dollars, and that looks like a fortune to us. He is quite an expert with a shovel and I think has an unusual gift in recognizing water ways and water resources.

We drive and ride often on the bench land that gives us a splendid view of the Snake River Valley, and he never fails to tell me that sometime there will be a railroad through the country. He says in ten years, but it seems to me it would be a very foolish railroad indeed that would come into this endless stretch of sand and sage-brush.

Can you fancy you see your little grandson number two, nestled here in the hollow of my arm as I write? He is one of the two finest boys in the world and how I wish you were here to help me love them. What a shame that you who love little ones so should be deprived of enjoying these. Oh, if you could just reach out your hand and touch the soft little black hair that covers this baby head. He has only a scanty wardrobe and every day is wash day at our house, but he is normal and healthy, so I am content.

With love from your three,
Emma

George Thompson,
Emma's father.

Unexpected Visitors

Blackfoot River, Idaho Territory
May 15th, 1872

My Dear Father:
Another spring has come to us and brought with it another of your letters. Surely I shall never be discouraged with such a father to send messages of cheer. The winter passed rather uneventfully as I am learning they usually do on Idaho ranches, but we all kept well and therefore, happy. Our little new baby never saw a white woman for a stretch of five months. He did not seem to mind it however, and when the first mild days came I carried him in my apron down to see my aunt where she and Uncle were building fence, and he screamed with terror at the sight of a strange woman. I hate to burden you with these things, but Aunt has never been to see me and I felt she must see the baby for she is the nearest to you that I have, but oh, so different!

The winter was uneventful but the spring, the spring has been wonderful! We have had guests, distinguished guests from the big world itself. You see there is a land to the north of us, perhaps a hundred miles, that is considered marvelous for its scenic possibilities and the government is sending a party of surveyors, chemists, etc., to pass judgment with a view to setting it aside for a national park. Well, this party happened to stop at our little cabin. There were representatives from all of the big eastern colleges, and then besides, there were the Moran brothers. I think you must have heard of Thomas Moran even as far away as England, for he is a wonderful nature artist. And his brother John is what I have heard you speak of as a "book maker." He writes magazine articles. And these two remarkable men were interested in us and in our way of living. Think of it, Father! I took them into the cellar where I had been churning to give them a drink of fresh buttermilk and while they drank and enjoyed it, I was smoothing the rolls of butter with my cedar paddle that Nels had whittled out for me with his pocket knife. I noticed the artist man paying special attention to the process and finally he ventured rather apologetically: "Mrs. Just, would you mind telling me what you varnish your rolls of butter with that gives them such a glossy appearance?" I thought the man was making fun of me, or sport of me as you would express it, but I looked into his face and saw that it was all candor. That is one of the happiest experiences of my life for that man who knows everything to be ignorant in the lines that I know so well. I tried to make him understand that the smooth paddle and the fresh butter were all sufficient but I think he is still rather bewildered. And do you know, since that day, the art of butter making has taken on a new dignity. I always did like to do it, but now my cedar paddle keeps singing to me with every stroke, "Even Thomas Moran cannot do this, Thomas Moran cannot do this," and before I know it the butter is all finished and I am ready to sing a different song to the wash board.[7]

Yes, I am doing washing now and earning money so I have every reason to be happy. There are well-to-do Southern families at Eagle Rock, eighteen miles away, and Nels drives there with the pony team and brings their washing for me to do. It is not hard and they appreciate having me do it for they have always had colored folks to wait on them and are very inexperienced and helpless. I thank you Father for bringing me to the wilderness when I was young enough so that I have been able to grow up useful. I am surely sorry for people that are not able to help in the world's work when there is so much of it to be done. The neighbors, the few scattered ones we have, are prone to criticize the way we get along, they say I make the living and a few such unkind things, but there is no work for Nels without he goes away from home, and I will do anything rather than have him go. I know how it looks to them, but I want you to understand that I am not complaining. Nels has faults, but indolence is not among them. He is really so very energetic that the task of "waiting for something to turn up" makes him quite irritable. I think, take it all around, though, that we are as happy as most people and the children are surely a great comfort to us both.

With our best love,
Emma

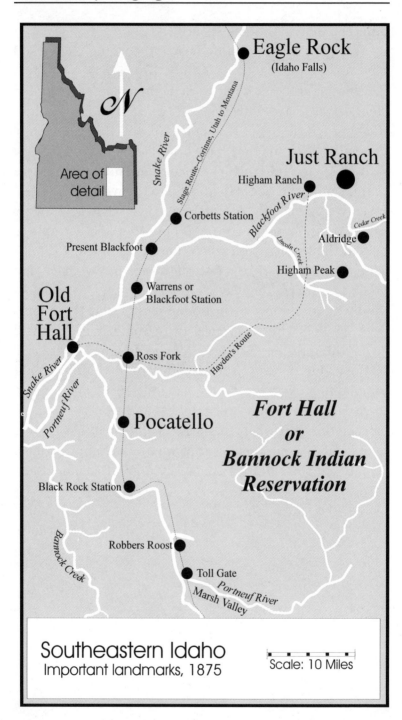

Eagle Rock
(Idaho Falls)

Just Ranch

Higham Ranch

Snake River

Stage Route–Corinne, Utah to Montana

Corbetts Station

Blackfoot River

Cedar Creek

Aldridge

Present Blackfoot

Lincoln Creek

Higham Peak

Old
Fort
Hall

Warrens or
Blackfoot Station

Ross Fork

Hayden's Route

Snake River

Portneuf River

Pocatello

Fort Hall
or
Bannock Indian
Reservation

Black Rock Station

Bannock Creek

Robbers Roost

Toll Gate

Portneuf River

Marsh Valley

Southeastern Idaho
Important landmarks, 1875

Scale: 10 Miles

Area of
detail

N

A Terpsichorean Episode

Dear Father:

Your washerwoman has become a slave to frivolities and no doubt the children will be going hungry in consequence. Yes, I have really been some place and that some place was a dance. The officers at Ft. Hall gave a general invitation to the settlers for a radius of sixty miles to come and make merry with the people at the post. I had very little hopes of going, for my husband cares not a thing for anything of that nature, but all the time I kept wanting to go, yet dreading to urge it. During the afternoon of the eventful day, a young couple who live at the stage station drove over and wanted me to go with them. My heart was in my throat because of my eagerness to go and my dread that Nels would be displeased with my going. Finally he came in and said with all the kindness in the world: "Emma, I know you want to go to that dance, go right along with these people and I will stay with the children but be home early." Oh, how happy I was! I knew that everyone in the valley would be there and such a celebration it would be! I had but one dress that was the least bit respectable and it was only calico, but it was nicely starched and ironed and being sort of a buff color, I thought, would be just the thing for evening wear. The truth is Father, it did not matter much what I had to wear, just so I could go. So all went lovely. The music was good and everyone was delighted to see everyone else, so we talked and danced, then talked and danced some more. I don't believe there were more than twenty women there and it took them all to fill the floor, they ranged in ages from twelve to sixty, but there were no wall flowers. After midnight, I began to get anxious to start home, but I could see that it was plainly an all-night affair. The only preparation on the part of the man that had so kindly taken me was, he was getting too drunk to drive. At two I was on the floor in a quadrille, when a hand touched my shoulder and my husband was saying: "Emma, your baby wants you." I vanished like Cinderella herself might have done. Someone took my place in the set and we were on our way without bidding anyone goodbye, without thanking any host, just on our way back to the baby. Our progress through the night was not rapid, for Nels had ridden a mule, that being the only animal kept up. I rode him and Nels walked along side of me. As we came over the last rise and found the cabin all safe that held our precious boys, dawn was breaking in the east. We had had a night of it. My husband's father has been with us all during this summer and he has built an addition to our house. A nice little "dobie" bedroom on the south end. Why, we feel quite aristocratic, for we no longer sleep in the room where we do our cooking.

We have had one unpleasant experience since I wrote last. Nels and his father had been cutting hay on the other side of the river and wanted to haul it over and stack it. The water was quite high and the crossing none too safe, so as Nels attempted to ford, one of the horses

saw fit to balk right in midstream. He could see that the
delay was going to be his undoing, so he jumped for his life
and let a goodly portion of our earthly possessions float
down the river. He managed to get out on the home side of
the stream and came rushing to the house, hatless and
dripping. "Well, here I am, Sis, but the team and wagon are
gone to hell," is the way he greeted me. Needless to say, my
heart was too full of thanksgiving to spend much time in
useless regrets, for little as we could afford such a loss,
how much less able we'd have been to lose him. It was not
such a complete loss, anyway, for I went back with him and
we found the entire outfit lodged. One horse was drowned,
but the other had kept itself up on the dead one, so we
rescued one horse and most of the wagon and harness. That
evening I returned the scare he had given me with interest.
We had been working on the other side of the river and
Nels told me to come to the foot log and wait for them to
help me across. It was growing late and there were the
cows to milk and supper to get, so I decided in the face of
the disasters of the morning, it would be easy for me to
cross the foot log. The foot log, however, was scarcely more
than a pole and one end of it splashed down into the same
surging water that had taken our team, but my courage
was up. I took the baby first and told Freddie if we fell in
he must wait there until his Dad came. When I landed the
first time I took the baby well back so he could not creep to
the edge and was soon back with the big boy. I went merrily
home and had supper ready when Nels came in, white and
ready to faint with fright. "Don't ever do that fool trick
again," was about all he could say, for it had been a day of
trials for him. Never had it occurred to me that he would
be frightened. I thought I was doing only my duty, but I
know that the foot log is almost unsafe for a man and I am
usually rather cowardly about water, as you will remember.

Maybe I shall try the ocean next if you do not come to me. I hope you are as well as this leaves us.

With love from,
Emma

Fred Bennett, age 13.

Hope Turns to Despair

My Dear Father:

The months have passed and I have neglected you. Neglected writing to you, but oh, never neglected thinking of you! Day after day thinking of you and praying that in some way your love for me will guide me aright. I have tried to write cheerfully to you, but if something should happen to me before we meet again, I should like to feel that you understood. Sometimes in the months just past I have felt that I might lose my mind, or even lose myself in the friendly river that I once feared. There must have been a growing dissatisfaction somewhere concealed in my heart almost from the time of our marriage. You remember, I told you it was not through sentiment that I married Nels but because I considered it the sensible thing to do. Think of it father! Think of trying to found a home without that prime essential, love. Of course I tried to be reasonable and think that romance for me was a thing of the past. I tried to believe that my love for Freddie's father was the only love that was ever to come into my life, but I failed to take into consideration that I was only twenty-one years old, so I cast my lot in the wilderness with a man for whom I could never feel anything more sacred than respect.

When the spring came, the third since our marriage, I concluded it was a hopeless task and I would put an end to it. Yes, I was going to run away. I had friends everywhere that would consider such a course praiseworthy. So my plans were all laid, even to giving up my little boy. I could not take Jimmie from his father, so I steeled myself to leave him as a sacrifice to the man I had wronged. I was to go with the older boy to the nearest county seat and secure a divorce, which is a very easy matter, then go farther east where I have friends. I was to leave all this barren life and go where there was civilization and cheer. I was to go where there was something besides hard work and where sometime the love of my womanhood might come to me! The love that is called the grand passion! The love that makes life worth while!

So I went along making my plans to go, counting the hours until I should be free, and trying not to look backward. Then one evening, I know not why, perhaps you sent the guidance for which I had prayed, but be that as it may, I told Nels all about it. Told him just as I have told you. Poor, poor man! What a shame he couldn't have been spared the suffering that I have caused him. Of course, he acted like a madman for several days, then lapsed into melancholy. Now, we are plodding along in the same old way, only with the knowledge that I have ruined all the chances for happiness that we ever had.

I am still doing washing for diversion and it matters little how many tears drip into the suds. Our evenings are spent in the gloomiest of glooms and Nels often says with a sigh, "My idols are clay." It is awful for him to have been so disappointed and it is awful for me to have been the cause.

Now, there is to be another baby. Another one to share our unhappy lives. I am glad for my own sake, but what of the child!

It seems almost criminal to me, for a woman to bear children by a man she does not love. Yet every day there are hundreds of babies born into homes where there is nothing but discord. Surely the world is nothing but discord, take it all-in-all.

Oh, father, do come back to us! Can't you dispose of your interests there and come back to stay? With your wisdom, perhaps you could straighten out some of the tangles in our lives. It seems to me that no lesser person could ever bring harmony into our discordant lives.

The children are well and are becoming quite good play-fellows now. Jimmie has golden curly hair and it makes a queer contrast to his black eyes. I thought when I began to write that there was not a thing in life for which I was thankful, but I know, when I speak of Jimmie, that I am glad I stayed to be his mother.

Your unhappy,
Emma

The Coming of the Peacemaker

Blackfoot River, Idaho Territory
May 5, 1874

Dear Father:

Another member has been added to our household, another boy. This time I was not disappointed with a boy, in fact, I rather rejoiced. There are so many things some of them very unpleasant, that boys escape by the natural order of law and life, so henceforward boys will be very welcome. Sometimes I think now that I never want a girl. My own life has been so full of blunders and mistakes, why transmit such tendencies to another generation!

Anyway the little chap is named for you and for Uncle William, George William, and he loves his grandfather already, though he is only a month old. He brought a great peace with him and it has settled over our little home with an air of permanency. I feel more certain of our happiness now than I have ever felt since our marriage. Values for me, seemed all upset for a while; now they have taken their proper places. I have ceased to long for the things that I felt so necessary to my happiness and I am learning to be happy with what I have. Nels, too, seems to have been chastened by my dissatisfaction of a year ago and is more considerate and thoughtful.

This time we were not alone to welcome the little stranger. A woman from the stage station was with us and it was most fortunate for I was sick several hours and not as able to help with the baby.

My good Heneage had expected to come and stay with me for a couple of weeks, but her brother Dick took suddenly sick the day she had planned to come. You remember, Dick was never a very strong looking young man and he had a stubborn case of typhoid fever. A doctor from Fort Hall waited on him and he had the best nursing that this country affords, but he died after suffering about three weeks.

This is the first death in the valley and it strikes very near to us all. I did not go to the funeral for my baby was very young, but they buried him in a corner of his father's claim not far from the Snake River. It seems very lonesome here to be among the first settlers in a new country, but what must it be to be the first buried in a new country! I shudder to think of it, and I hope that the song of the river reaches the lonely spot where he sleeps.

Father, would you believe that your "washer woman" has a wonderful new piece of furniture? A sewing machine! Think of it! The simplest Singer on the market and it cost $72. I told you that I was earning money of my own by washing for the Andersons; well, my first earnings paid for that. It was freighted with an ox team from Corinne to Eagle Rock. It surely is an acquisition and my friends come from miles around to have me sew for them. They gladly do all of the drudgery around the house if I will just condescend to put machine stitching on their hems.[8]

We also have a glove-making job that seems to have quite a fortune in it for us. The Andersons supply us with buckskins, thread, buttons, etc., and we make the gloves for 75 cents a pair. In this work Nels is able to help me a great deal. He does all of the cutting out, then I do the work with the machine and he turns and trims them. Lastly I finish them by hand. We often complete three pair in a day, during our leisure, and that seems like making money pretty fast to us. Most of it has to be done at night after the children are in bed. We burn two tallow candles and it almost keeps one of us occupied keeping them "snuffed" so that they will give a good light.

Being a "shop keeper," perhaps you will like to know more of the glove industry. The skins make on an average, three pairs of gloves each, and they bring from $1.50 to $2.50 per pair, the price being regulated by the quality of the buckskin. How do you think they would sell to your London customers?

Sometimes I get a chance to make a pair of buckskin pants for a trapper or miner, they have to be lined and are quite difficult to make, but I get $5 for making a pair. Once I was making some for a man that was riding with my husband and wanted to get them done while they were away. In my eagerness, I cut both sides for one leg, so, of course, spoiled two fine skins—skins that did not belong to us, too. When the man, who expected his pants to be ready to wear said, very slurringly: "Yes, I've always heard a woman can throw it out of the window with a spoon faster than a man can throw it in the door with a shovel," I was just ready to cry real angry tears, when Nels came to my rescue by saying: "Never mind, Sis, we'll get two more buckskins and you can make two more legs to go with the two you already have." We did and soon found sale for the second pair, so there was nothing wasted.

The baby is waking and the cows are coming home to be milked so my letter must be brought to a close.

With the love of your three grandsons and,
Your Emma

Sickness Comes in the Wilderness

Blackfoot River, Idaho Territory
February 15, 1876

Dear Father:

How easily we may say or write "we are all well," and it seems to carry so little meaning, but henceforward it shall always be the most meaningful sentence in the language to me. For I have learned what it is to be unable to say it! I have learned what it is to watch and work and wait by the side of a little sufferer until I was almost frantic, searching for one ray of hope. I have learned what it is to go night after night without closing my eyes until I ceased to feel that sleep was a necessity. Yes, father, I have learned a lot of things.

Early in September our little golden haired Jimmie was stricken with a terrible fever, something of the nature of typhoid, yet the doctor gave it some other unpronounceable name, and for four months he lay, feeble, moaning, unconscious. After the first few days he never recognized any of us, but would open his mouth like a little bird when anyone came to the bed. Every two hours we fed him from a spoon, either medicine or liquid nourishment, and every six hours bathed him.

Some days I would feel hopeful and meet the doctor with, "Oh, he is better today, doctor," but the doctor would look at him and shake his head. His solemn "No change" would shatter my rising hopes. I have never lost a child but it seems to me that we must have suffered more than we would to have really given him up. There was his pitiable little skeleton ever before us, almost accusingly, as much as to say we were not doing enough; there was the endless, nerve racking care of him, and there was ever the conviction that we must lose him after all.

We had some help with the nursing. Aunt came, and dear Heneage Garret, who was just married to a young Southerner, forsook her husband for a few weeks and came to us in our need. We had a woman from Fort Hall, too, for a time, but four months is a long time to worry through, and much of the time we two were alone fighting for that precious life. Even little Freddie has had to be enlisted as washer woman and I shall long remember his faithfulness in washing little garments, at the same time amusing Baby Will by letting him "fish" in the tub with a tiny pole and line.

We never really knew when the change did come, but gradually, so gradually, he began to mend. Then, we were able to release the doctor from his self-imposed contract. He had made over a hundred trips on horseback, a distance of 22 miles, and we poor, poverty-stricken home-builders had only one hundred dollars to offer him for all his wonderful services. Goodness I hope if heaven is crowded, that all the rest of humanity will be cast out to make room for the doctors, doctors such as this one. We asked him his charges, and he said, were we able to pay, five hundred dollars would be the least he could ask, but knowing our circumstances, he wanted nothing. Think of it, father! And yet some old cronies will tell you that the world is getting worse and every second man you meet is a scoundrel. I've never found it so. We insisted, however, that he take all we had, to prove in some measure our gratitude to him. I even said, "Why doctor, you have saved our child," and he came back with "Saved your child, no, my good woman, all my knowledge of medicine could never have saved that child, had it not been for your nursing and your strict observance of my directions. Doctors could save a great many more children if they were only blessed with mothers like you."

So after nearly half a year, our sunny little boy has come back to us. He learned to stand again, and to walk the early part of this month. He has been eating solid food, tiny strips of dry toast, piled high to look like a great quantity, and he has grown fat like a little baby again.

Once more we sleep through the night without interruptions, once more we listen to three peaceful little breathers, instead of a moan. Once more we are happy in our cabin home.

With our fondest love,
Emma

Another Son

Blackfoot River, Idaho Territory
September 30, 1876

My Dear Father:

It must be almost on old story to you now to hear that we have another boy at our house. Anyway, another one we have, born the sixteenth of this month. You no doubt are keeping count and know that he is the fourth, but do you realize that your "Little Gal Em" has more of a family than her mother ever had? It means a great many responsibilities and a great many duties, but I still feel equal to the task, if I could just be sure that four would be all. Surely no mother should be called upon to wash and cook and sew for more than four. Surely not a mother who is called upon to do for them so early either. Yes, again we were alone to welcome the little mite.

I think I told you that Mrs. Shoemaker is ailing a great deal so she keeps a girl year in and year out. She is a faithful Danish girl that would be a substantial addition to any household and Mrs. Shoemaker had promised to let her come to me when I needed her. Nels and I drove down expecting to bring her home but the Shoemakers had suddenly discovered that they could not spare her.[9] Of course, there was no time to make other arrangements, after depending upon her until the eleventh hour, so we came home a pretty blue pair of expectant parents. Before morning the baby had arrived. We took care of him just as we did little Jimmie, Nels acting as a surgeon and I as a nurse. Sometime during the most exciting times Nels moved the stove in from the little shanty kitchen where we had done our cooking during the hot weather, and had it in readiness for the newcomer. Poor little fellow, his coming did not disturb many people, but he seems as happy and healthy as if he were a prince and welcomed by a whole kingdom full of people. We have named him Francis. I had always hoped to have a little girl to bear my mother's name, but it has begun to look as if we never shall, so he may have it.

You asked about school for the children. It seems about as unattainable as the moon and I must confess that I have not given it any very serious thought. What is it the Bible says about "Sufficient unto the day?" Each day brings so many cares that I cannot look far into the future. Sometimes I wonder whether we are going to be able to subdue these conditions enough to produce the necessities of life for our ever increasing family. Of course, we are teaching Freddie to read in the evenings. The books you have sent and a few given to him by friends here are supplying endless entertainment but when I really think of an education for them, here in the wilderness, it frightens me.

My first work now, when I am able to work again, will be to make winter suits for three little boys. There is no store to buy material from and no money to buy it with, but frequently men who are traveling through the country will leave an old pair of pants or a badly worn shirt and from them comes a new suit. Nearly every thing worn here is good wool and when the old garments are washed and pressed they look like new. I suppose the little chaps would look very different from the ones that pass your shop window, but I try to keep them warm in winter, cool in summer and tidy all the year around.

The poor youngsters were the innocent cause of their mother being foolishly offended once during the winter. A sleigh came with bells, a most unusual occurrence, in fact I think it had never happened before since we have lived here, and the children in their mad rush to the door fell over each other or over the chairs. Anyway when the occupant of the sleigh came in they were all crying. He remarked very pleasantly that he always found when a stranger stopped at a ranch house, there was a kid crying in every corner. I answered him very sharply that we only had three children so there was not one in every corner. I hope he does not come this way again, partly because I did not like his impertinence, and partly because I do not want him to know that there is one in every corner now.

There seems to be a little dissatisfaction among the Indians and it worries the settlers. Up to the present they have never shown anything but the most friendly attitude, but we hear vague rumors of uprisings among the tribes to the north of us and we fear it may extend to this reservation any time. I have never feared them because of our experiences with them that winter at Soda Springs. They might so easily have wiped out that little handful of us, had they cared to do so. I think in most cases, the white folks are at fault when any difficulties arise. However, we are not always our "brother's keeper," else we would surely try to keep him from doing imprudent things with regard to the Indians, and thus be assured of their good will. [10]

We have all been exceptionally well during the summer and hope when your precious letter reaches us it will bring as good tidings from you.

With love from all,
Emma

Francis, age five, and William Just, age eight.

Charles, age two, and James Just, age 11.

The Red Man's War-Whoop

Blackfoot River, Idaho Territory
September 14, 1877

Dear Father:

Tell me, Father, is it a mark of insanity for one to wish to take his own life? My husband says it is, but I insist that it is perfectly sensible, so we shall expect you to cast the deciding vote. I have been on the point of killing my children and myself that we might be spared a more terrible fate, and before you agree with Nels that my mind is becoming unbalanced, I want you to know how logical it all appears to me. I think I must have mentioned our fear of an Indian uprising when I wrote last. Well, with the coming of spring our worst fears were confirmed and the summer has been a season of terror. I often wonder if some of the newspaper reports reach even to where you are and if you picture us, your very own, being burned to death in the little cabin as you read of a lonely habitation being destroyed.

The Nez Perce tribes to the north of us with Chief

Joseph as leader have been doing depredations of all descriptions, and each time we hear, coming nearer and nearer to us. Albert Lyon, whom you remember from Soda Springs days, was captured by them out in the Birch Creek country, which is only a hundred miles from here, and he barely escaped with his life. He was freighting with Green's outfit and when the Indians came upon them they took possession of the wagons and drivers but assured them they meant no harm, just wanted to detain them so that they could not give the alarm. After being held several days, Lyon managed to give them the slip by dropping into the wash then following down the bed of the stream, and finally reached a cabin in time to save himself from a death of starvation. His fellow travelers were all killed and the wagons burned before the savages moved camp. Some, who wish to promote a Christian attitude toward the red man, insist that it was because Lyon betrayed the trust, but it seems to me he simply saved his own scalp.[11]

But to return to my own story. Nels has been putting up hay at Fort Hall the greater part of the summer, often staying away over night. Brooding as I did, I could not sleep when alone and I dared not make a light for it would only serve as a target for some stealthy redskin, so all night my imagination ran riot. I would see through the windows bushes and stumps that were familiar to me by daylight, but by night they took the form of a crouching savage, of which there were a million more just behind the shadows, surrounding the cabin. Night after night I spent in that way, and day after day I milked the cows and made the butter with my head hidden away in an old slat sunbonnet, lest the children might discover my changing expressions.

When Nels came home he brought papers with vivid

descriptions of the path of terror the Indians were leaving in their wake and I felt positive that it was only a matter of time until they would join our own tribes here and complete the destruction of the white race in southern Idaho.[12]

The fall days began to come on when a heavy haze hung over everything, sometimes poetically called "Indian Summer," but that one word has taken the poetry out of everything for me this summer. Nels had not been home for several days and the desperation of continued loneliness was upon me, when toward evening the children came rushing in from their play to say there was a fire on the hill south of us. I tried to assure them that it was just something that looked like a fire, but I knew too well that it was a fire, a signal fire, that one band makes to let the others be in readiness for a celebration. That night I was almost frantic and while the children slept I made up my mind what I must do to save them. I resolved never to let them be mutilated by savage fingers before my very eyes. No, no! I had read of such cases and mine should never suffer so, while I was held captive perhaps to bear other children by the savage brute that had murdered mine. I had given existence to mine, now at such a crisis it was my right to take it from them. I would drown the older ones, one by one, then take the baby in my arms and go in beside them. To try to hide would be useless—the baby would cry and we would be found and tortured more for trying to deceive them, so with the first intimation of their approach we would find our only safety in the river so near at hand.

I felt perfectly sure that the end was near, the signal fire had been the culminating event in the tragedy, but after the children had eaten the breakfast which I was unable to taste, I went on with the milking, through force of habit, I suppose. I'd milk a cow, then go up the hill to strain my eyes for the coming of the enemy. At last I saw what I expected to see, a dust, or was it a smoke? In either case it meant the same. It was just at the point where the Shoemakers live and if it were dust, the Indians were reaching there; if smoke, they had been there and were leaving. There was no time to lose. I called my poor terror-stricken babies around me and told them we must all drown together. If the older ones held any differences of opinion, they knew their mother too well to express them, so with a board in my hand, on which was to be scribbled an explanation to Nels, we started to the river.

Like Lot's wife I turned once to look back, and the cause of the dust I had seen was in plain view—my husband. I have heard of the interventions of Providence and this must be an illustration, for in ten minutes more he would have been a man without a family. He called me crazy and said he would never trust me alone again and I am not sure that I blame him. The solitude must be getting on my nerves. I need a neighbor. I need companionship. I never seem to feel lonesome for I am always busy, but I have had too much of my own society.

He brought the word that the wicked Nez Perces have swerved back to their own reservation and our own tribe is in the most peaceful frame of mind so we can feel relieved until the green grass starts again.

Little Francis is a most remarkable-looking child. Weighed twenty-seven pounds at five months old. I don't know that he is any more healthy than the others have been but he is a picture of contentment. He is so large that he is inactive and will sit for hours in one place, just being good.

I hope this recital will not worry you, Father, since it

has all passed into history before it is ever written, but I want you to know how terrifying it really is, so that you will not blame me if I ever do have to kill the youngsters to outwit the savages.

With all our love,
Emma

A New Friend

Blackfoot River, Idaho Territory
April 3, 1878

Dear Father:

The spring has come again and found us all here enjoying the best of health. I rather imagine that my last letter has disturbed you a good deal during the months that you have not heard, but I have not had occasion to threaten the lives of my poor youngsters again.

We have had more Indian scares, too, but I have had pleasant companionship and the river has been frozen over, two good reasons for more deliberation.

A woman with two small children, acquaintances of ours, who live over on the stage road, came over to stay with us while she had a felon treated by the doctor at Fort Hall. The felon was a terror so she was here many weeks and what had been a mere acquaintance has ripened into a friendship that I am sure will be enduring. She is such a calm, patient, Southern woman, quite young in years but so old in experience. She came west as a bride. Not a particularly happy one either for the marriage had been arranged by her elders without her consent. After struggling along for several years, she left the husband and came to the stage station near us to work and earn a living for herself and little boy. She secured a divorce and all was going well for she is such a competent woman, then one morning while the little boy was playing in the yard, two men came driving by and while one leveled a gun on the door of the house where the mother was at work, the father of the child picked him up and took him back to Virginia. So my poor beautiful friend was alone in a strange land. Later, she married a man much older than herself and they have two children but she is not happy. The West is so unkind to its women. I know how she longs for her Southern home and for her first-born. It seems, with so many men to choose from, surely there must be some good husbands but I see so many failures all around me.

With all our winter has been pleasant though. After the felon had given us all the trouble it could, the doctor concluded he would have to take the thumb off, so here in the wilderness I have had a little experience in surgery. Joan was quite sure she would be alright if I would promise to stay with her and all during the time she was under the ether, she kept saying, "Are you there?" and when she knew I was she was contented. By the time it came to the tying of the stitches she struggled so that the doctor asked me to tie them while he held her and I did. So you see, my first experience has not unnerved me to any great extent.

It was during the time she was here that we had our bad Indian scares. The first time a messenger was sent out from the Fort to warn the settlers. He surely warned us in a manner that strikes terror to my heart to recall. About midnight, he dashed up to the door and yelled: "Look out for your hair, the Indians are coming!" and was gone. Frantic with fear, we bundled our sleepy youngsters up and started for the Fort eleven miles away, expecting any minute to be cut off from help and murdered. Well, it wasn't so bad after all. The worst feature being that as soon as we reached the Fort in safety, Joan discovered that she had left her purse, with quite an amount of money and some valuable rings in it, lying on the bed at home, so Nels turned right around and went back for them leaving us there in safety. He was not gone long and we all remained there for several days until the excitement had died away. The real cause of the alarm was that an Indian, thought to be insane, had killed two white men down near Ross Fork, then when the sheriff came to make the arrest, a young man named Alex Rhoden pointed out the offender to the officer, and he too was shot, so it made a lot of feelings and a general uprising was feared.[13]

A second time they sent out messengers from the Fort to rout us out of our beds and tell us to fly for our lives, the second time we did not fly. We just reasoned that we were taking more chances traveling eleven miles that hour of the night than we would to stay in our own home. It just seemed that if we were to be killed, we would be anyhow, and if not, why bother?

Anyway the unpleasantness is all forgotten in the memory of my new friend. I shall never forget her patience and her fortitude. Many a woman with such an affliction would have considered herself an invalid, but not she. She helped me with the work in so many ways and took care of her children so much better than some women do who are all sound. Poor dear, so often in taking care of the baby, she would get the thumb kicked or bumped, causing her untold misery but she never complained.

We have entered into a financial agreement that is almost causing me sleepless nights. We have never had a great supply of this world's goods, but it has always been our own. Now, we have gone in debt. Nels bought a beautiful, brown mare from a man of means at Malad, and paid, or promised to pay, $250. The note will not fall due for a year but I cannot be sure just where the money is coming from and each day I am afraid that something will befall her and we will be obligated to spend the rest of our lives "paying for a dead horse" as the saying goes.

I often think of your simple little method of avoiding the credit menace in your shop. You wrote me once how you considered it better to give a small amount, explaining that the money should be brought next time, than to extend any credit. I hope for my own peace of mind that we will take the money with us the next time we go to buy a horse.

With love from all,
Emma

An Addition to the House and the Family

Blackfoot River, Idaho Territory
December 25, 1878

My Dear Father:

Christmas finds us this year with one more little boy two weeks old, and a new room added to the two that have served us so well. Again I have had a morbid determination to put an end to all this struggling, for each year seems to bring so many new burdens and each year I seem a little less able to bear them. When I first knew there was to be another baby, I went to Nels and told him that I thought I had better drown myself and was very much astonished that he should disagree with me. There I had carefully figured out to my own satisfaction, thinking that perhaps he could raise the four, but if there were to be more and more of them, more than I could make clothes for and more than he could buy clothes for, what was the use! Someway he scolded, threatened or begged until I consented to stay a little longer and we are quite happy now to begin another winter.

I guess Nels concluded too that there was not much room for number five, so during the good weather he has built on a nice big room, in fact, it is two rooms. They set the new one with a space between it and the original house, then filled in the space making a sort of hall so it really gives us four rooms now.

Another thing that has given us a little comfort, we have had a Missouri family living with us since September and she is very good help. I had a very bad sick spell in the early fall and we heard of these people rather by accident. He had been freighting and she was living at Malad so we got them to come here for the winter. They have one little boy and we let them live in one of our small rooms, so that our housekeeping is separate and yet she helps me whenever I need it. She is a forlorn, homesick creature and I think her misery helps me to see the folly of my own ways. She is always grieving to go back to old Missouri and cries most every day. In fact her tears have become so common with us all that my husband offered her a quarter to laugh once. The offer was so ridiculous that she did laugh. Poor Mollie, she has enough to cry over if there was any hope of tears bringing a change. Her husband is a good deal older than she and none too kind. She came out here away from all her relatives to make a fortune, I guess, and the fortune seems very slow about materializing. They must have been raised in the most benighted section of the South for they use awful English and he cannot write his own name, but they have had their church and their camp meetings and they miss all of those things. We were amused at her a short time ago. We butchered a hog, the first since they had been with us, and she exclaimed in the most delighted manner: "Oh, good, at last we shall have some meat!" We nearly always have fresh beef and frequently fish and game, but with her, pork seems to be the only thing that counts as meat. Well, with all her peculiarities, she is a good-hearted person and has certainly been a blessing to me.

My, my, I am almost forgetting to tell you about the baby's name. Our little Willie boy, who is now nearly five and very witty, bought him from this Mrs. Warren soon after his arrival for twenty-five cents and named him Charlie. I do not know just why that name or why his fancy for it but we all think it a pretty good one.

And our Freddie boy has become quite a fisherman. In fact, I almost feel that my occupation is gone for he is quite as successful as I, even when I have the time to give to it, and I seldom do these busy times. During the summer, it was quite a common thing for him to go over to the river for an hour or so before supper time and come back with as many as he could carry.

Jimmie seems to be the worker of the flock. He is all business. Goes with his father to chop or shovel and seems to know just how to do it all.

I believe I told you when I last wrote that we had contracted our first debt. Well, we paid it in six months instead of a year and were not obliged to pay any interest, but I hope we never, never buy another thing until we have the money to pay for it. I fear and despise debt and I hope that my children, my grandchildren and my great-grand-children will do the same. My first home might have been a happy one had it not been for debt and drink. It only takes one of these destroyers to wreck a home. But to return to the mare. Nels had wintered a lot of freight oxen, that is he had kept track of them for the owners, while they ate Uncle Sam's grass. That netted him a neat sum. Then we have had some government contracts supplying beef to the soldiers at Fort Hall and that has given us quite a substantial lift, so the mare is paid for and she has a beautiful, mare colt that is the pride of the family, so I guess, she was a good investment.[14]

I don't believe I have ever told you of the queer, or perhaps I should say "large" experience that we have had in the soap-making business. During a period of several months, or possibly a year or two, of butchering, we had accumulated four hundred pounds of tallow. Nels hauled it to Corinne and could only get four cents a pound for it, so he brought it back and we made it all up into soap and candles. I don't think we will ever be out of soap. May have to ship you some to sell for us.

Well, I have written away the daylight of a short winter afternoon and I hear a stir in the cradle where my tiny son lies sleeping, so good-bye for another time.

Our love to you,
Emma

The Witness Stand

Blackfoot River, Idaho Territory
March 8, 1879

My Dear Father:

Here I have been so busy relating the details of family
life that I have forgotten to mention the coming of the
railroad. When we settled here, my husband always said
there would be a railroad in ten years and his prophesy
has been fulfilled in about seven as it reached the little
burg of Blackfoot fifteen miles from us, sometime during
December. Now, I've had a ride on the steam car. Would
you believe it? And a visit to the city of Zion, the Zion that
you brought my mother six thousand miles to see.[15]

It is very changed since I saw it last in the sixties, but I
took little note of its improvements for my mind was too
much engrossed in the three-months-old baby in my arms
and in the fact that I was the star witness in a murder
trial. Can you imagine it Father? Your little Em taking
such a part in the affairs of men.

I did not realize that my testimony was of such vital

importance until it was all over, then the remark of the attorney was heard to the effect that I was the one witness they feared, but wait, I have not told you. One cold night in February a very unusual looking man appeared at the door and after making several inquiries, drew out the subpoena that called me as witness on the trial of Robert T. Burton being held on the charge of murder at Salt Lake.

In the years of our trials of homesteading, I have tried to forget the details most unpleasant of all our early experiences, the Mormon-Morrisite war. As I have grown more mature in judgment, I have realized that we poor misguided Morrisites were very much at fault, for in defying the sheriff's posse as we did, we were really defying our government, for even though the posse was formed from the pillars of the Mormon church they were vested with the authority from Washington and we should not have tried to evade arrest. But this is all looking backward and I must proceed with my adventure.

Of course, first of all, I protested that I could not leave my family but Nels said it was my duty to go and he felt sure that my memory could not fail to bring the guilty to justice.

So I went but with a sinking heart! I regretted to leave my four boys that I had never been away from over night; I regretted to take my tiny infant among people where might lurk the germs of every dread disease; and I regretted most of all, going among the Mormon people. They say a burnt child dreads the fire, so I guess a child that has been shot at cannot help fearing the hand that pulled the trigger. Every foot of the way we traveled I expected the train would be blown off the track, for it carried a number of witnesses, or I expected we would be burned in the court room, anything to wreak the Mormon vengeance as I had known it. But the Mormons are changed since those days, Father, they are a different people.

Still, frightened as I was, when I sat in the witness chair the old scenes came back to me as vividly as if they had occurred but yesterday.

I saw the hills blackened by the approaching enemy, heard the bugle call, our own beloved Morrisite call, that assembled us in the bowery and I knew again with what joy and trust I went forth expecting to be delivered by the hand of the Almighty. Then I saw a cannon ball come rushing through that humble gathering, fired by the waiting hordes on the hillside, and two of our trusting Morrisites lying dead in the bowery. Yes, I saw it all, father, and told them as only one who had seen could ever tell it, and the Mormons assembled there in the name of the law, began to fear me just as I had at first feared them.

I told them of the babe in its mother's arms falling to the ground at the boom of the first cannon and before the firing ceased, falling again when its second protector was killed. I told them of a woman, then in their city, who had lost the entire lower part of her face when the first ball was fired into that defenseless gathering of men, women and children.

I told them of the hoisting of the white flag by our terror-stricken band and of the Mormon warriors, less heeding than any savage tribe of the wilderness, continuing to fire, killing four right under the flag of truce.

I told them how, on the second day, I had gone skipping across the public square in childish fearlessness with "cannons to the right of me and cannons to the left of me" to find my mother huddled in the little cellar under our house, white as in death, marking the number of cannons fired with a stick in the dirt. She had counted seventy-five that one day. Oh, Father, I can see her always, poor suffering creature, as she took me in her arms saying: "Thank God, my child, you are safe." I looked at her in childish eagerness and dismay saying: "Why, mother, is your faith weakening? God will punish these foolish destroyers." But she only hugged me closer sobbing: "My child, bullets will kill!"

I told them how after three days of almost continuous firing, they had surrounded us taking our men prisoners after having killed our beloved prophet, Joseph Morris. I told them how in the struggle that followed his fall, you stood by the lifeless form of the prophet and said to the Mormon that had once posed as our friend: "You've killed him, now you better kill me." And of his attempt to shoot you had his gun not refused to obey his will. Then I told them of the gentle creature, Mrs. Bowman, who came forth during the struggle calling one of the leaders "A blood-thirsty wretch." I told them how, before my childish eyes the fiend exclaimed: "No woman shall call me that and live." and suiting the action to the word, he shot her down.

And so after all these years, I was the instrument to avenge these wrongs to what mild extent it could ever be done. I was in the witness chair and my word would send to the gallows the murderer of that poor woman.

After questioning me sufficiently, they asked me to look around the court room and see if I recognized anyone. Did I? Well, I certainly did, just as I would recognize you, my own father, after all these years of separation. There he sat with his same flowing beard and gleaming eyes. His face had been the one thing that I could see distinctly all during my examination, as it had looked when I saw him years before and as it looked then. I think it had really served to bring the scenes before me more vividly as I recounted the details, particularly when it had come to the point of his pulling me roughly away from the body of Joseph Morris just after I had seen him slay Mrs. Bowman, but at this point my memory only served to set him free.

You father, no doubt would have remembered correctly, but the two leaders, Stoddard and Burton, had always been pointed out to me together and just as sometimes will occur, I had transposed the names, and the guilty man that I saw before me was the one I had always believed to be Stoddard. It so happened that the man Stoddard had been dead a good many years, so my testimony simply laid all the crimes on to the dead man and set free the criminal before me. So ignorant was I of courts and counsels, and so dependent upon my childish recollections, that it never occurred to me there was any chance for mistake until I had killed my own evidence.[16]

Anyway, I was glad to be through with it and be free to come back to my little boys and my home. I had been gone for two weeks and had never heard a word for each day they expected I would be back. Each day Nels had sent a team to meet me only to find a letter saying the trial dragged on. I guess it seemed long to them but it was surely an eternity to me, and I have never smelled anything so sweet as the sage brush that crushed under the wheels that night when they brought me home. It was a mild spring night and had been raining so that everything was fresh and pure in such contrast from the coal smoke I had been obliged to breathe. I found everyone well though the children had been sick during my absence and we were a happy family indeed to be reunited. I think that home coming will always stand out as one of the happiest times of my life and in spite of my failure as a "star witness." I hope this letter will carry to you a portion of the contentment that is in my heart.

Always the same,
Emma

The Coming of the Londoners

Blackfoot River, Idaho Territory
June 3, 1879

My Dear Father:

Next to seeing you, I cannot think of anything that could
have given us greater pleasure than to welcome the two
splendid young men, Arthur and Lewis Judges, that you
sent to us. Such an event to have two nifty Londoners arrive
at the humble dwelling of the Justs on the far-away
Blackfoot. If they had but waited to get our letter of
instructions they might have been a little better prepared
to meet the conditions that now confront them, but they
have such a wealth of enthusiasm that such things as
suitable wearing apparel are really minor considerations.
I must say though, that even amid my joy at seeing them,
there was an undercurrent of regret that our home is so
dull and dirty. I guess woman was ever thus, but I seem to
be spending my life waging war against dirt and yet it is
everywhere I look. But it is the boys I want to tell you
about. Surely you did not know what an amount of arms

and ammunition they burdened themselves with. Such a picture they presented when the liveryman dropped them down at the door, dressed in the styles of the old world and then duly protected against beast and savage by every known make of fire-arm. 'Tis well that we have a Post near us for I imagine that in a very few weeks they will have many army supplies to dispose of.

Fortune favored them, for in a day or two after they came, a young man who works for us came driving a bear up to the corral. Their plan was to butcher it in a most dignified manner, after getting it gently into captivity, but the new-comers rushed out and frightened the poor beast so he trotted up above the house and they over-took and killed him. We rarely see one these days and certainly are not often on such familiar terms with them but I think this one must have put in his timely appearance just to give the boys something to try their guns on.

We've had another experience, too since they came, that almost proved the death of me, that is, if humiliation ever does kill. I began to cut the boys' hair, you know, of course, that I am the family barber, and the first one I looked at was lousy! Think of my children being lousy! I called in another one and he was lousy, and then their father, and he was lousy, and I didn't know what to do. I had never seen a head louse since the early days in Utah when the school children all had them and I remember how horrified my mother was when she found them on me. She thought it was the worst disgrace imaginable because in England only beggars had such things. Now in our home we were over run with them just at the time we most desired to be clean and respectable. I begged them all not to mention it to the Judges boys for I knew it would be the one thing they could not forgive.

We held a family council and decided that the young

man who had come to work for us had brought them to us, so we called him in to have his hair cut, but neither louse nor nit was to be found in his head. Then they all washed with strong home-made lye soap and we hoped we would be rid of them. All promised well until my husband insisted that the Judges boys be told of it, said it was their right to know for they might catch them. The children were having a lot of fun over the discovery. They thought the little creatures very interesting and it was very hard to keep the matter hushed so finally it all came out and the immaculate Englishmen decided to have a turn at the hair cutting. Poor fellows, their equipment for the wilds had not been sufficient to protect them from everything; they had more than anyone, lice and nits of every description. In the fair haired boy's head, the lice were light colored, and in his brother's they were dark and it was evident that they had brought them to the ranch for they had more than anyone. We supposed they had picked them up on the ship or on the train, but they, of course, had never seen such a thing. So we are rid of them now, I think, and the tenderfoot boys are becoming westernized.

Some things are so hard for them to understand, the dryness of our air and sunshine is one. I had washed a few things for them one very warm day, and as I gathered the clothes in early in the afternoon, I folded their night shirts, rough dry, and put them in their room. That evening, Lewis came out and said: "My word Mrs., I would not dare wear this night shirt, in England we would not think of wearing our clothes without they were properly aired." I didn't laugh, honest I didn't, but I did want to ask him what he called that stuff that was circulating around our clothes line all day, if not *air*. They are such fine chaps though and they will learn some day that whatever else we may be short of, we have great quantities of air and sunshine.

They will stay with us until they make some definite plans for themselves. Our Missouri family moved away this spring so it leaves me the burden of work again. Arthur is just like a girl having done nothing but indoor work and he is very handy about helping me in the kitchen. He is also starting a garden and my little boys are so taken up with him.

Baby Charlie is growing and well and he joins the rest of us in sending his love to his far-away grandfather.

Your
Emma

A Tragedy

Blackfoot River, Idaho Territory
December 6, 1879

Dear Father:

Our beautiful baby boy was so terribly burned a few weeks ago and I hoped by waiting I might be able to write you that his little features are not badly marred, but sometimes I feel there is no hope. He was sitting in his high chair, near the stove, and I had a coal oil can of water heating so I could not see the baby from where I stood and by some means the chair in which he was sitting tipped over throwing him on top of the hottest part of the stove. He struck his face on the side and then slipped so that the skin was just simply taken off the whole side of his face and the inside of one little hand that reached out to try and save himself. For two hours he screamed with us walking up and down the floor with him, the only thing that we could do until the doctor was sent for by messenger eleven miles away. Finally he went to sleep and the left eye swelled so that we never expected that he would open it again. Of course, it was very little that we could see when he was in such agony, but we felt sure the eye ball was so injured that sight would be destroyed. The doctor came and dressed the burns once and since then I have taken care of them myself but the poor little mite has suffered terribly. He was such a good baby and his features all so perfectly formed, you know what a beauty he is in the little picture I sent after we came from Salt Lake, it seems such a pity that he must grow into manhood scarred because of his parent's carelessness. The eye is all right but at the corner by the temple the lid droops and there seems to be the deepest scar but everyone thinks that because of his being so young much of it will grow away.

I suppose we should be thankful that we have been so fortunate thus far with our family, no broken bones and only the one seriously sick, but the thing that hurts us most with this, we shall always feel that it should have been avoided. As in all accidents, no one knows just how this happened but there must have been something under one leg of the high chair so that it did not set level for it was never known to tip over. Really the chair is quite the pride of the household. Grandfather Just made it for Jimmie and it has the sturdiest look as if it would protect a baby from anything. The legs are well apart so the base is wide and it seems the next thing to impossible to upset it, besides, it has helped a great deal in bringing three baby boys safely to little boyhood and we cannot understand how it happened to fail us with the fourth.

You will be anxious to hear from the Judges boys, I know. Arthur is still with us and will teach the boys this winter. They will work in forenoons and then have school in the afternoons. It is a very happy arrangement for us all and the boys are eager to begin. Lewis tried several things, among them cowboying, and had his face so blistered that he scarcely knew himself. It was evident to us that he had been too long an indoor man to make a success of any sort of rough work so we persuaded him to go to Salt Lake and try and find employment. That is the nearest point where a bookkeeper could be sure of finding work, but he was loath to go because of the Mormons. He said: "Drat them, I won't work for them," but he knew that our advice was for his good so he finally swallowed his prejudices and went. I wonder, father, if you are responsible for his animosity toward the Mormons? He is surely very bitter but if nothing else he will find their money quite acceptable and I am sure they will find his services the same for good office men are not easy to find, even in Salt Lake, and the Mormons are obliged to secure much of their help from among the Gentiles for their converts are mostly from the uneducated classes. Still the Mormon people as a class have made great strides forward since you knew them and when you come back, which I hope will be very soon, you will not recognize them.

We have instituted a system of starting the boys in the cattle business. Each is to be given a heifer calf when he is ten years old, then he owns the herd that will accumulate and he will feed them. We also pay them a certain amount for such chores as they are able to do, milking, wood chopping, churning and such things, then they buy their shoes or something that they need with the money. We hope it will teach them something of the value of money but it is hard to tell just what to do to be sure of making good useful citizens of them.

Fred has had a saddle pony of his own for some time and he adores spurs, bridles, saddles and all that pertains to horses and the stock business in general.

I must go now and look after my poor little suffering infant.

With our love,
Emma

A Neighborhood Wedding

Blackfoot River, Idaho Territory
June 1, 1880

My Dear Father:

The winter passed rather more pleasantly than usual. The boys were so interested in their first school, the baby's scars are becoming dimmer each day and everything seems to be running very smoothly.

For real winter diversion, we had a wedding. Our neighbor, Mr. Burrell, who has long been a confirmed bachelor, took unto himself a wife on New Year's day. They came by in what seemed to us grand style, four horses and a hired driver brought them up from Blackfoot where the ceremony had been performed. The bride comes from the States but has been in the Malad country some time nursing. She is much younger than Mr. Burrell but had been married before. Nels is not on good terms with Mr. Burrell, they have had difficulty over lines and cattle, in fact, most everything, so I have not been there, but Arthur Judges visits them and tells me about her. She is very lonely as I can well imagine, with only one neighbor and she not allowed to visit. Well she and I cannot quarrel as our husbands do if we never meet.[17]

I tell you so many of our troubles that I sometimes wonder if I give you the impression that we have nothing pleasant to record. We surely have. One of the great events is our yearly pilgrimage to the Stevens ranch. Of course they only live about twenty miles away but there is always something to be done, cows to milk, butter to churn, etc., and to neglect them might mean starvation, so only about once a year do we all don our best clothes and go there to stay over night or perhaps two. The children look upon that trip as sort of a combination of Christmas, Fourth of July and picnic. I guess I have failed to tell you that there are four Stevens children now. The second, a girl named Emma for me, then a son, Jimmie and a baby girl, Abbie. They usually visit us about once a year, too, so that the children keep well acquainted. Her Fred and my Fred also write occasionally. Oh, yes, you spoke of our Fred's penmanship. Isn't it remarkable? Why, when he was nine years old he could write so much better than I that I refused to write copies for him. Does it ever seem to you that such a thing as penmanship could be hereditary? I do not believe much in heredity but I do not know how else to account for his gift. You know what a wonderful artist his father was in that line. Why I have sat entranced, watching him write out the great long muster rolls in the army and the motion of his pen was like the strokes of an artist's brush. That father never saw the boy since he was five weeks old, yet here he is writing with everything and on everything, imitating every new hand writing and at the same time developing one of his own that positively resembles his father's even now.

There is another form of diversion we enjoy during the

pleasant weather. Early some Sunday morning we drive over to Sand Creek, about five miles, and camp. The ducks are plentiful there and while Nels rustles enough for dinner I give the boys each a hair cut, then they bathe in the creek, put on clean clothes and we come home at night, refreshed and ready for work again.

We do not raise much yet so that the cattle are about our only income. Of course the garden helps and we raise enough potatoes to last us through the winter. We have planted a few acres of alfalfa, or lucern as we prefer to call it, but it did not yield very well and the grasshoppers played havoc with what did grow. The water is still the big problem and Nels is always planning and working to get the water on a larger acreage. Most of our land can be irrigated in time but it is too big a job for one man in one life time. He has had to hire some help already and the ditch they have dug is only a sort of an experiment. We have set out a few fruit trees with the hope that we can get water enough to them to keep them alive. Our old friend Billie Jones of Ogden sent them up after seeing me in Salt Lake at the trial. Even a fruit tree that may never bear looks a little bit more like civilization.[18]

Sometimes it seems like a terrible struggle and we wonder if it is worth while, then again we feel full of courage that we will win in time. Once Nels was ready to move to Montana and give it up but I persuaded him to stay on a little longer and I don't think he has ever regretted it. A spot that is none too fertile but that is home is better than beginning a life-long search for the "promised land." Once a traveler stayed over night and looking over the situation said: "Why don't you folks go back to Missouri where you can raise something?" One of us made answer that we were afraid we couldn't make a living. "Pshaw!" he said, "anyone that can make a living *here,* can any place." So we are none too prosperous but we owe no man and we are here first so whatever opportunities a new country has to offer we are here to accept.

My duty calls me so with fondest love, I must say good-by,

Emma

When Death Comes

Blackfoot River, Idaho Territory

My Dear Father:

I cannot tell you when I wrote to you last but it must seem very long indeed to one waiting in loving anxiety. I do know, however, that for a year now life has been sort of a cruel nightmare to me and I had no desire to share my trials with you. Sometimes I have thought that the worst must be over, that our lives would be easier for the rest of the journey, but I know now that the past year has been the hardest of our experience and I do not seem able to rise above it. I am broken in health and my mind is a mass of chaos. Five little boys are hourly needing my attention and I haven't the strength to give them any. Day after day they go with buttons missing and faces unwashed and I can only look on in despair.

You see, last April we were expecting a baby and were again confronted with the problem of securing help, so late in the winter Nels happened to run across a young woman at Blackfoot who was in need of a home and thought we could manage to help each other. She had a young baby and was living with relatives, her husband having left her rather mysteriously soon after their marriage. All promised well enough but she was young and inexperienced and with the baby to care for, so I soon found that instead of help, I simply had two more added to my family. It was not long though until a strange man appeared at the door way to claim a wife and baby and explain that he had been terribly sick some place away off the railroad and had not been able to write to her. They were soon a reunited family and after she did up his accumulated washing and gathered up her few belongings, they started out for themselves.

By that time we were getting in desperate need of help so we sent up Snake River, to a place called Conant Valley, for the Missouri couple that had been with us before.[19] They came as soon as weather and road conditions would permit, but our children had already begun to fall sick. At first we thought it some simple malady but they seemed to have such terrible sore throats, so we finally called a doctor from Fort Hall, and horror of horrors, he told us we had scarlet fever of the most malignant type and emphasized his decision by saying he would much rather his children have the small-pox. We never go anywhere to expose the children to disease so we knew it had been brought to us by the father of the baby, for our boy that had taken a special fancy to him was the first to take sick and the last to get well. I remembered too that while his wife was doing his washing there was a most peculiar odor rising from the tub.

So for three weeks preceding my confinement, we had six children down at once, five of ours and one of the Warrens who had come to help us. Twenty nights I took my turn sitting up half the night, then when I knew that I, too, must soon be a care, I finished out the night. And the next day, just across the hall from my little boys moaning in their delirium, I gave birth to twin girls. We had an old Midwife and she gave us the best care she could, but it was poor enough and I think both the babies and myself had the fever. The doctor told me I would take it but I was determined to stay with the boys until the last. Somehow we all struggled through but the babies were always puny. One weighed six and one seven pounds at birth but they never gained the way they should. I did not have enough milk for both so gave them part cow's milk and the hot weather was too much for their feeble little bodies, so in September they both died, just five days apart. We had named them Finetta and Heneage for my two best friends and they lie buried on the bench that rises north of the house, just far enough over the brow of the hill so I cannot see the graves from the door. Their little coffins had to be made of what materials we could find for we have been at such an expense. Some of the time we have kept help in the house but my Fred boy has been my one faithful helper through it all. It does not seem fair to burden one so young with such a weight of cares but there seems to be no other way.

During the life of the babies, I slept with both of them and with little Charlie, who was just past two, and Francis in a trundle bed by the side of me. Nels felt that he could not be robbed of his rest or he would be unable to carry on his work, so for the five months I had the care of the four and I never knew what it was to sleep two hours at a time. Then when I could see the first one failing I was reconciled that she must go but I was sure that we would raise the other, and even after she died, the children and I consoled each other that the cradle was not empty as it would be in most homes when a baby had died. But when the second one had to go, all that I had borne during the months seemed to crush me. When I looked at her little dead face I wanted to scream and run away from it all, then just when I would have broken down, Nels put his hand on my shoulder and said: "Bear up, Emma, for my sake." Bear up, I surely did. For weeks and weeks I never slept a night and everyone feared I was losing my mind. It seemed to me that I had no mind to lose. Nels would take me for long rides in the buggy or on horse back, miles and miles and miles to try to tire me so I would sleep but the nerves that had been strained so long would not let go. I have seen him hold a ticking watch at my ear for two hours at a time with the hope that the monotony would bring me sleep and rest, but sleep was, or seemed to be, out of the question and all the time I had never shed a tear over the loss of my darling babies. Oh, Father those dreadful weeks are too terrible to recount.

I am better now. That is, I am sleeping better, but the reason is that there is to be another baby. It must be Nature's way of bringing me rest but it seems like a very queer way. I shall be glad to have my poor empty arms filled again, the spirit is willing but the flesh is so faltering. When I look at my five poor little neglected boys, I wonder why Nature doesn't see fit to send them another and more able mother instead of sending me another baby. Here am I who was once able to do work for others and bring in money, unable to care for my own house and children. I must not trouble you longer, father dear. I think I am really glad now that you live so far away you have been spared much.

With our love,
Emma

Another Little Grave

Blackfoot River, Idaho Territory
December 12, 1882

My Dear Father:

I've had another promise of a daughter—only a promise
and I have but an empty cradle and an aching heart to
remind me of the hope.

Somehow I dragged through the weary months of
summer but about a month before we expected the baby I
realized that something terrible was wrong. I had not over-
exercised nor over worried but I knew that the life had
gone from the body beneath my heart. I knew that my own
body that had been a temple where reposed a precious life,
had suddenly and mysteriously been transformed into a
morgue. And oh, the gruesomeness of that certainty!

I told Nels of my fears but I could not convince him
that it was anything but "Woman's imagination." I begged
him to call a doctor but he did not see any need of it. I
guess I should not blame him for how can any one but a

mother know what a difference there is between a living child, with its sensitive little muscular body responding to her every emotion, and the leaden weight of a child that no longer moves? To him duty is everything and he strives to do his full duty but there are times when a little tenderness would count for so much more, and his indifference at this time I feel was one of the cruelest blows he has ever dealt me. Days that seemed as long as years followed one after another and I waited and worried. Finally he began to feel alarmed and called a doctor. Of course, the doctor confirmed my belief. Told us just how long the baby had been dead and when I could expect my delivery. After that I waited again but I did not worry so much. To know the worst is better than uncertainty, and I knew that it was going to be a fight for my life and I must prepare to meet it bravely.

Just at the time the doctor had specified, I was taken sick and the baby, a little girl, was born within a few hours. I never even looked at her for I needed every atom of strength and courage to aid my recovery. They buried her immediately beside the other two, so I have three little girls, but they are all "gone before."

The much-feared complications from such an experience, never came, and I am in as good health as I have been for some time but if I could petition the Powers-that-be I should say, "Spare me from another still birth." Surely it is enough to ask a mother to put her life in the balance for the sake of another life, but to suffer the same agonies and only be rewarded by another little grave, is unbearable.

I have this one consolation now, however. I have nothing to fear in the years that are to come. I can rest in the assurance that life has nothing worse in store for me than it has already handed out. Within two short years we have had three births and three deaths. Disease has laid us all low and robbed me of the strength of my young womanhood. I can surely stand anything after what I have been through.

I have help in the house now, a very good girl, though only fifteen years old, and she is good company for me, too. Our family is large this winter, we have a cowboy boarding here and Nels has a miner named Frank Gary helping him with the rock work on his ditch. In order to get water on a large portion of our land a ditch must be taken from the river half a mile farther up, then a bluff, or outcropping of lava lies directly in its course. That must all be blasted away. These bluffs occur at regular intervals all down the widening river valley, one near the house we have used for the north side of the corral. So one proved very useful and the other has to be removed by a slow and laborious process.

This Mr. Gary is also quite intellectual and is continuing the boys' schooling in the evenings, so all promises well for pleasant winter after the turbulent seasons that have passed into history.

With our love,
Emma

The First Circus

Blackfoot River, Idaho Territory
September 4, 1884

My Dear Father:

When the weeks and months pass by rather uneventfully I grow careless about writing and the first thing I know a year has passed. I am glad that your letters to me come more regularly for what could I do without them?

I know you will rejoice when I tell you the youngsters have been to a circus. The first one that came through the country stopped at Eagle Rock and we all went to see it, that is Nels took us up and we made a little camp just outside the town and he stayed with the team while the children and I went in. He imagined that the horses might get frightened of some of the animals and get away from us. I really do not think he cared to go anyway. We've lived in the silent places so long that it is very hard to adjust ourselves to noise and crowds. A crowd there certainly was! Hundreds of people from hundreds of miles around! There was a time when we knew most everyone in this part of the valley but the settlers have come so fast since the railroad got here that we cannot keep track of them.[20] I was not able to enjoy myself much as I was afraid of an accident, but five small boys had the time of their lives. Fred got away from the bunch and caused me a great deal of anxiety, but during the performance, a clown did something funny trying to imitate one of the others, and just as Mr. Clown fell, I heard Fred laugh away up on one of the highest seats. A circus costs a lot of money for a family the size of ours but it was worth it to see how happy the boys were.

I am glad you asked about the Judges boys. I believe I told you that Lewis went to Salt Lake City. He had no trouble to get a good position there and soon was installed in the Z.C.M.I., which is really a mercantile establishment conducted by the Mormon church. He soon married a Mormon girl, too, so his extreme prejudices were forgotten. Arthur went from here to the Stevens ranch but has left much of his London learning with the boys. He taught both their heads and their hands. He was such a wonderful gardener! Why, he raised tomatoes and other tender vegetables such as we imagined belonged to tropical climes. It begins to look as if we had been so busy making a living we have never found out what a wonderful country this is.

Once while Arthur was here, he borrowed a catalogue from our new neighbor, Mrs. Burrell, and we send there for almost everything we use. Prices are so moderate and the joy of ordering and receiving goods right in your own home are not to be overlooked. The boys are just about beside themselves with joy when a bill of goods arrives from Montgomery Ward.

Another source from whence come our earthly goods is an Irish peddler who makes yearly trips through the country. Besides the goods that he sells he holds us spellbound until far into the night telling us of his travels. He has been everywhere and is a good talker so we watch eagerly for his visits. He usually plans to spend Easter with us and he is as welcome as the spring itself.[21]

I must tell you, too, that I have met Mrs. Burrell. After she had lived within a mile of us for more than a year, she came down one morning to tell us that a deserter had been seen in their field. He had gotten away from the camp at Ft. Hall and she knew that the searchers were here. I've also met her since at Mrs. Warren's. Guess I've never told you that the Warrens finally located on the river above Mr. Burrell's. So even though Mrs. Burrell and I do not visit, in deference to our husbands, we each have a friend in Mrs. Warren. Often when my work is done, I take a horse and go for a delicious little ride up there about two miles, and after a few minutes talk with her come back refreshed and happy.

The boys are getting to be more and more help to me. Fred has recently taken over the washing for men that happen to be here. He buys the soap from me and they pay him a small amount for washing so he has a little profit besides taking that much work from me. They're good boys but I wish they would not quarrel so much. I tell Nels I know that other people's children don't quarrel so much as ours, but he thinks I am mistaken. Why, ours even quarrel after they are in bed when there is nothing to do but sleep. One time I was so desperate with it all that I rushed in to Nels and woke him up to tell him I wished he would get up and let them yell "Dad, Dad" a while, for it had been "Ma this, and Ma that" until I was nearly frantic. He woke up startled and said: "Why Emma, you'd be out of luck if they couldn't yell 'Ma.'" Of course I cried, the only thing there was left to do and I always felt it was a just rebuke. Surely the knowledge of the little graves up on the hill should make me kind to the ones I have left.

Another time when I had been tried to the limit of endurance, I concluded to send Fred away from home, so I packed up his few belongings and started him down the road. Of course, I kept hoping he would come back soon and he did very penitently. Raising boys is certainly a problem. This leaves us well though, and small matters of disposition do not matter so much.

With love,
Emma

Another Little Sister

Blackfoot River, Idaho Territory
August 8, 1885

Dear Father:

Yes, there has been another little sister at our house, just loaned to us for a few weeks, then taken away to join the other little sisters who are never to grow up. I do not see why it had to be for her chances seemed to be so much better for life and health, but I am beginning to feel that we are never to have a sister for our boys. Five boys and never a sister for them! It seems to me that I have but two wishes: One is to have you safely back to America and the other is to raise a daughter. Always I keep hoping but the years go by and neither prayer is granted. The boys are almost men now and no one knows what a power for good a little sister would be in our lives.

This one was born when it was summer, June sixth, and we had good help. The country is full of help now. There is no more dread of being alone with sickness. Several Scotch families have moved in from the mining towns in Utah and there are two lovely girls named Mackie that take turns helping me, then a woman of much experience was here to take care of the baby. She was very kind to me and I felt that all would surely be well this time. The baby, too, seemed perfectly normal at birth, she was such a darling and looked as if her eyes were going to be blue, but by the time I was able to be up and around, I fancied that she was not gaining as she should, then she seemed to just fade away. Each day the change would be so slight that no one else could notice it and I felt it rather than saw it myself, then the day she was four weeks old she died.

I shall never forget Lizzie's kindness to me. It was the fourth of July and a young man had come to take her to a celebration. I hated to ask her to stay but I knew the baby was failing fast. She stayed gladly enough and it was only a few hours until the tiny life passed out. We had named her Frances Ella, so my mother really has a little name sake, and the Ella was given because of a very dear friend we have had in recent years, a friend that came here often from the little town of Blackfoot and laughed with us or cried with us as the mood suited. She was a wonderful girl but she too has gone, back to her home in Illinois.

I guess that one can even become accustomed to death. It is beginning to seem that way with me. I am not in the terrible broken down condition that I was at the death of the other babies, anyway. My health is very much better, of course, than it was at that time, and this has been the longest rest I've had between birthdays. I do not dread the coming of another though when I have lost one. Gladly would I have one the next day after one has been taken away. Nobody knows what the loss of a baby means to a mother. Every minute of the day and of the night I miss her. Nels and the boys come in and look at the empty cradle with a pang, but when they go out, they forget while my loneliness is always with me.

My Fred boy has been working away from home now some for two summers. He is herding horses now for the Stevens people. Gets fifteen dollars a month and he put his first three months' earnings into a saddle. I am not sure that he is going to be any better at saving money than his father was, but I guess we should not expect our children to be better than their parents in all respects. If he will only keep away from strong drink I think I can stand most anything else, still I must admit that I was very much shocked a short time ago when I heard him use his first swear word. I do not mean to infer that it was really his first, most boys sound such forbidden words before they are sixteen years old, but it was the first time I had heard him and I almost fell over. His one desire is to be a cowboy and I may as well be willing. He does not take to ranch work the way Jim does and I guess I should feel very well satisfied that he has stayed with his step-father this long. I am not sure though that parents are ever satisfied. I fear we all expect too much.

We've had one of Nels' brothers with us since I wrote last, Peter, the youngest one. He came riding up, all unannounced, and asked if Nels Just lived here. I said: "Yes," and walking a little closer to the horse, added, "and you're a Just too." He smiled an awful broad smile and said he did not see how I could tell. Of course, I had never seen him but I knew him from his resemblance to his mother and you know, I had seen her twenty years ago in Soda Springs. He stayed with us several months and their father came down from Montana to see us while he was here. The father and mother have long lived apart so Peter went back to his mother in Nebraska.

Must close with the hope that the years will soon be bringing you to

Your Emma

What Civilization Means

Blackfoot River, Idaho Territory
February 1, 1886

Dear Father:

In the days when we first located here, I used to sigh for the things of civilization. I thought it would surely be a joy to be able to purchase the necessities of life without traveling for days and days. I thought it would bring better schools for our children, better care for our sickness, in fact, better everything. But I find it is like everything viewed from a distance, it is not at all what I expected. True, we have a few little towns that have sprung up along the railroad, where they sell dry goods in very small quantities and wet goods in very large quantities. Once we had only space and sunshine, now a thousand temptations appear for my growing boys.

We've had some of the evils of intemperance brought to our door recently and it makes me wonder if I am someday to find myself the mother of a drunkard. There had been a Captain Baker stationed here at Ft. Hall for a time and later removed to Ft. Douglas. He had friends here and some property, so he came up on a visit and began drinking and gambling at the little town of Blackfoot. I don't know just how long it had been going on but Nels happened to be in town one day and a mutual friend suggested that he bring the Captain home with him to try and sober him up. So on the pretense of buying some of his horses, Nels brought him home. Poor, miserable piece of humanity! The night before he had made out checks to the amount of fourteen hundred dollars to pay his gambling debts and after he began to get back his reason Nels offered to go and stop payment on the checks, but being a thoroughbred, he declined the offer saying: "If I was fool enough to write the checks, I can at least be man enough to pay them." He stayed with us several days sick in body and mind and we did everything we could for him for we realized that he was the kind that was worth saving. He was a trusted officer in the Rebellion, a man of much learning and refinement, yet he had gone to the lowest depths. One of the many interesting experiences that he related was the capture of Wilkes Booth, who had murdered our beloved Lincoln. He was a sergeant of the squad that overpowered him.

We do not know that he has mended his ways, but he left here the most grateful person you ever saw and he has shown his appreciation by sending us loads of reading matter, magazines and papers from all parts of the world, and then at Christmas time such a wonderful gift. It is a breast pin, I guess, but very large, and was made to order by Joslin and Park, the leading jewelers of Salt Lake. The design is a sword with the belt, straps and buckles, all complete in gold, of course, but so perfectly engraved that you forget it. The first thought is that it is large and clumsy but the more you look at the fine workmanship the more of a prize it becomes and it seems such a fitting gift from a

Captain to the wife of a soldier. Nels has always been a trifle jealous of my enthusiasm for things military, but his love of the beautiful is so strong that pettiness is forgotten and he joins me in gratitude for this wonderful gift. I just believe that when you come back from England I will meet you at the gate with the little green velvet box for I am so proud of my one piece of jewelry.

I wonder, sometimes, whether I am as thankful as I should be for having a husband that does not drink. When we were married it seemed to me that all other faults were as nothing compared with that one great fault and if Nels would not drink I could forgive everything else, but pshaw! of what value are such promises to ourselves? Now that he has proven all that I expected in that one particular, I find that I would like him to be different in a thousand other ways. Why, I want him to always be kind and always be thoughtful! It does not seem like it is asking much either, but he isn't always kind and sometimes we quarrel over trifles and make our lives very miserable. Why must folks go on doing what they know is wrong, else why should they strive to do better? It may be that I expect too much, for the men of your generation, Fther, kicked their wives about when the occasion demanded and the poor wives felt lucky if they did not get a down right thrashing, but here I am pining because of a few cross words. It has always been my boast that we have never disagreed on the three big issues of life: religion, whiskey and the children, but everything else under the sun has given us material for argument. Then after arguing for a while we quarrel, then say ugly things and I cry and Nels goes away disgusted with me and with life in general.

We have never had any difficulties over other women, but Nels is not the lovelorn youth that I married. I overheard him once telling a young man that he had to lie to a woman to get her and I wondered how much of the love he professed for me had been just to "get me." I was scrubbing the floor at the time and I added a lot of tears to the scrubbing water. And such is life.

Why burden you with matrimonial difficulties, you've had your share and you will rejoice with us that we are all well and prospering, so what else matters?

With love,
Emma

A Little Sister

Blackfoot River, Idaho Territory
February 1, 1887

My Dear Father:

Can you believe it, we have a tiny baby at our house, a girl baby? She was born last September but I never had the courage to write the good news to you for fear, well, for fear that before the letter could make its long journey to you, our joy would again be turned to mourning. I have so been obsessed with the feeling that I was never to raise a girl that I hardly dare take my eyes off this little mite lest something will befall her.

Now she has been with us nearly five months and seems as healthy as a child can be so perhaps I am to keep her after all. Perhaps I am to raise her to be a useful woman, a companion to me in my later life when some of the struggle and hardships are past. In the last few years I have maintained a sort of training school for girls and I find plenty of mistakes that other mothers have made in the training of their girls, now I shall have a chance to try on my own. I have had sixteen-year-old girls come to help me, grown young women and perhaps contemplating matrimony, who could not make an apron or a batch of bread. What were their mothers thinking of to raise girls that do not know how to do the commonest little duties of everyday life? What kind of homes will my boys have when they marry such girls! But, of course, my girl will be different. While she lies there in the cradle I can imagine great things for her.

She came when the leaves were getting ready to go, when the world was full of golden sunshine and golden leaves and the heavy blue haze hung over the mountains. I always think that our falls are the best part of the year, now I know they are for this one has brought me the daughter for whom I have longed. My fifth little daughter, my five in one. Now, if I can just live to raise her and to see you again. I shall feel that life has been indeed kind to me.

For help this time we had a young Scotch woman who just moved here from the mines in Wyoming. She and her husband are homesteading over on the railroad and as she has only one little girl, can get ready in a moment or two. Nels went for her after I was taken sick and my Jim boy was with me, the other Mackie girl, Agnes, was here as my regular help. Nels was not gone long and Mrs. Kerr is a woman of experience in all lines so everything went pleasantly. I had planned to have a doctor this time but we got along very well without one. When the baby was a few hours old, my good helper, Agnes Mackie came and held her on her lap and I suggested that she name her. She said that she did not know any good names and I asked her what was the matter with her own name. She modestly protested but I assured her that it was a good name to me, so Agnes it is. I can imagine you will soon be writing letters to her. This Mrs. Kerr has a beautiful little daughter named

Maudie. She has such wonderful golden hair and the bluest of blue eyes. She looks like a doll or a fairy here among my dark-skinned boys, but they are very fond of her. She is as good as she is pretty and she may always be attractive to my swarthy boys but she is only four years old now. One of my favorite theories has always been that babies should not come into homes where there are grown up children, and where the older children are beginning to have babies of their own I have looked upon it as a positive disgrace. I used to sometimes even wonder if my own grown-up boys could love a baby, but when my big Fred boy came home to see his little sister and knelt down beside the bed to love us both, I knew that she was not "one too many" as I had feared. Oh, how they all love her! Some people are already predicting that she will be "spoiled" but I refuse to be her mother if she is. I shall expect her to mind just as her brothers have done before her. Of course with so many brothers she could be spoiled but I shall make it a point to see that she is not.

This has been the coldest winter of our experience, during the entire month of January the mercury has registered below zero and there is a lot of snow. We have sold hay to sheep men and they are feeding here on the river but the severe weather is hard on stock of all kinds.[22]

I must close now with five big loves from five big grandsons and one little, tiny, tiny love from one little granddaughter.

Your
Emma

Agnes Just as a toddler.

Agnes Just at 18.

Just family ranch house in 1890

The Big House

Blackfoot River, Idaho Territory
January 15, 1888

Dear Father:

This year has been spent mostly in building. Did you ever imagine that your little "Em" would be living in a brick house by the time you made her a visit? Well, the brick house is assured and the visit we are still hoping for.

We have only one room finished but it is such a big kitchen that we live in it and get along very well with our sleeping rooms still in the old house. You see we have burned the brick right here on the place and the lumber is hauled from saw mills in the mountains so it has been a long job requiring a lot of labor. Then too, we are trying to have it all done as cheaply as possible for it is making terrible inroads in our savings. It is built very much on the plan of the old house, so we will not feel too much like visitors. The long kitchen occupies the entire west side of the house and the front will be toward the east with a hall to the kitchen and large room on one side and two small ones on the other. There will be a loft where the boys can sleep and the stairs lead up from the hall.

My good Nettie has a new house this year, too. Such a beauty. It has a parlor and dining room and all such things that belong to the world of civilization, and a lot of fine furniture that Steve has shipped from Ogden. Bureaus and wash stands with solid marble tops. I never saw such pretty things and I count myself fortunate indeed that I am privileged to visit there and enjoy it all. Everything of hers far outshines mine, of course, but mine are still very much better than I ever expected to fall to my lot. In all our years of friendship I do not think there has ever been one shadow of envy or jealousy. We have always rejoiced in each other's good fortunes. I would as soon think of envying Nettie her beautiful golden hair, as her finer home. Why I remember how we all adored Nettie and I think I loved her more because of her prettiness than for any other reason. She was fair and I so like a Gypsy. In fact, that was one of your names for me, "Little Gypsy," do you remember? Even Nettie's children, while I will not say they are better than mine, are far more gifted. I believe I love her Fred just the same as I do my own. He is such a wonderful boy. So kind and thoughtful and, at the same time, so intelligent. He is the greatest source of information. I always have a lot of questions saved up to ask him when we go down there, and he will answer them in such a kindly gracious manner that he makes me feel like I really knew it all the time and was doing him a great favor to ask him.

With the passing of the Stevens family into the new house, one of the old land marks is abandoned, the old log house that was hauled from Soda Springs and has been the scene of the happiest times of our lives. "Bummer's Retreat" the old room with the fireplace was usually called because everyone with time to spare congregated there.

How the old walls have often echoed with laughter and song after a sumptuous supper of corn meal mush and milk. I wonder if we shall ever be able to adjust ourselves to brick walls and marble-topped furniture.

With the children of the two families growing up in such intimacy I wonder sometimes if they will ever marry. It seems like it would be ideal for them to, but perhaps that is the reason they never will. Children seldom care to marry where it would be perfectly satisfactory with the parents. Well, anyway the friendship has meant a great deal to all of us in the years that are gone, and that is enough to know.

Our little girl is growing and walking but she does not talk yet. She uses a great many signs and gestures to make herself understood but seems very slow in saying words. I guess she will talk, though, if we give her time. Nettie has a baby boy a few months younger than Agnes, her fifth, but she has them all yet. So with new babies and new houses we are leading very busy, happy lives.

I must away to my countless duties, hoping this finds you well as it leaves all of us.

Your
Emma

An Irrigation Project

Blackfoot River, Idaho Territory
September 3, 1889

Dear Father

This is becoming such a busy world that I hardly have time to write to you and the first thing I know you will be thinking I do not love you.

Now that things seem to be getting pretty well done at home, with the new house finished and water on most of the land, Nels is undertaking something bigger. Water is to be brought from up the Snake River, above Eagle Rock, to irrigate a large amount of land that at present is worthless. The people who are doing it call themselves "The Idaho Canal Company" and Nels is interested both as a promoter and a contractor.

I am not sure that I approve of the step, but like most husbands he did not ask my advice. I've always looked forward to the time when we could feel that all the necessities of life were provided for us and we could have a little leisure for the things that we long to do. A rose bush or two that will bloom as if they enjoyed it, a strawberry bed where we could pick our own fresh berries, and even a good unfailing vegetable garden where we could be sure of finding good things to eat all through the summer. These things do not appeal to Nels. He always says: "Oh, Sis, never mind, we'll raise a ton of hay and buy all the strawberries we need." He is looking for bigger game.

Of course his vision is broader than mine. He sees what an enterprise like this will mean to the country, while I only see that it will take him away from home and burden him with a lot of work and worry. The ditch or canal is to be about thirty miles in length and will supply water for 35,000 acres of the finest land that ever lay out doors. Land that we knew to be superior to ours when we located here but we knew too that it was more than a one-man job to get the water to it. Not an acre of our own land will be benefitted by the new ditch but Nels feels that he wants to take part in making "The desert bloom as the rose." [23]

Another point that appeals to him. He has always maintained that a father with a growing family of boys should provide work for them or they will drift away from home. This is his opportunity. By taking contract work he is giving them a chance to do the work that they understand. We have not been able to give them much schooling so they must of necessity be sons of the soil, men that work with their hands.

Our Jim boy is such a wonder! He is really in charge of contract work and, though only eighteen years old, he has had as high as thirty-five men working under him. I wish every father and every mother in the world might have a Jim boy like ours. Such a boy in years but such a man in shouldering responsibilities. I can hardly remember a time when he has not been his father's most trusted helper. He is not very strong looking. I don't think he really ever recovered from his terrible sick spell, but his supply of energy seems to be inexhaustible and though small of stature his muscles are like iron and there never seems to be a job too big for him.

Will, too, is on the ditch job. I don't think he will ever have any executive ability but he keeps his end up at the regular work and part of the time he has been doing the cooking at one of the smaller camps. We happened in one day unexpectedly and found one of the nicest dinners ready. I couldn't have told but what I had prepared everything myself.

Even I have been called upon to help with the new work. At the big camp they have a woman and a girl doing the cooking but Nels thought they should have a few lessons from me. I was with them several days and quite enjoyed it. Think of bread mixed in a wash tub. The only thing that would hold enough for such a lot of hungry men.

Grandfather Just is with us again now. He has been in Montana a good many years but he feels now that he will need to be where someone of his own can take care of him. He eats his meals with us but has a little home of his own fixed up in a part of our tool house.

Wish us well in our new enterprise and come see us.

With love,
Emma

Presto

Presto, Idaho Territory
April 20, 1890

My dear Father:

Do you note that change of heading in this letter? Do you know what it means? Wonder of wonders, we have a post office. Our dear, kind hearted Uncle Samuel has consented to carry our mail for us, to bring it to our door twice each week. It actually seems to us that we are living in the very heart of civilization. The post office is right here in our own house, mind you, with Mr. McElroy, who is here teaching the children, as post master. The name is one Nels suggested to the Department and as you know, is Mr. Burrell's given name, but he and Nels are such enemies that Nels denies having any intention of naming the office for him. Be that as it may, it is a good name and a wonderful convenience to the neighborhood. It is a star route from Blackfoot.[24]

Another blessing has been bestowed upon us by our Government. To encourage the growth of timber on Western prairies, they have passed a law that by setting out a certain number of shade trees, you can acquire an additional hundred and sixty acres, over and above the homestead. Nels lost no time in availing himself of this opportunity. It is a lot of work but the reward is two-fold and I am quite overjoyed at the prospect of so many trees to beautify our somewhat barren homestead.[25]

You should certainly be glad to hear of one thing upon which we agree so heartily for I certainly recount enough of our disagreements. Most of our quarrels, fortunately, are over little things. I think we have had more difficulty over the sewing on of buttons than anything in our married lives. Different trouble than you might imagine, too. Some husbands complain because of buttons left off, but mine always has his trouble with the ones I want to sew on. If I see a suspender button missing or a wrist band hanging down, it is my natural impulse to rush to sew it on. I would gladly take my hands out of the dough or leave my dinner to get cold while I relieve him of the annoyance, but just when I think I am being most considerate, he scolds me for bothering, so the missing button ends in a quarrel. Once when we had jangled for several hours with such a small starter, Nels said in his petulant manner: "I don't see why you want to bother about such small things." In the coolest tone I could command, I said: "Well, if it is a small thing for me to bother with don't you think it is a pretty small thing for you to object to?" He hesitated a minute and answered very submissively: "Damn if I don't believe you're right."

Another of our pet subjects for argument is floor scrubbing. Nels is firmly convinced that a floor never gets dirty enough to need scrubbing, so I usually do it when he is away from home. When he comes back there is perhaps no supper ready, no cows milked, just a clean floor. Naturally he scolds me and, being tired and hungry myself,

I am very easily offended so in a very short time I am crying and feeling that he is a brute to abuse me so. Really the most serious quarrels have always been because he thought I was not taking proper care of myself so I guess they have not been very serious after all.

Our canal-building venture has had no unhappy consequences and they can see the end of it now. It has been a terrible strain on Nels for it has brought him into contact with other people of varying opinions. Up to the present he has had the chance to manage his work just as he saw fit, but with this he has found it necessary to give and take a good deal and the nervous strain has made him very hard to please with home affairs. Still I think it has been worth the price and the shares he holds in the company will give us a nice little income for our later life.

The last winter has been a hard one on the country. It put a lot of cattlemen out of business. You see, up to the present, the really big stockmen have made no provision for feeding their cattle in winter. Of course, the grass is good, wonderfully good, and by keeping a good force of men on the job, they could use the desert, the Ft. Hall bottoms, the foot hills and the mountains as the weather conditions best suited them. In that way they managed to bring them through without any great loss, but last winter was so very severe, with all their wonderful variety of range, there was nothing left uncovered and the cattle died by the thousands. The owners of them were living in luxury in their eastern homes, figuring on the number of steers they would have fat for the June market and before word of the distress could reach them their herds were reduced pitifully, or in many cases wiped out completely. This will mark the passing of the cattle king, and perhaps it will mark the dawn of a new era, the era of irrigation.

We are all very well now but my little girl is a constant

anxiety. I dread the coming of hot weather for each summer she has had such terrible bowel trouble that I've feared that I couldn't pull her through. Oh, I cannot spare her!

Write to me oftener now that I am so sure of getting your letters without any needless delay.

Love from all
Emma

Emma and Nels Just, 1901.

Counting My Blessings

Presto, Idaho
May 1, 1891

My Dear, Dear Father:

Can it be possible that this is the last time I am to write you! Can it be that after twenty-four years of cruel separation, we are to be together again? I am so happy I can hardly settle myself to write. It seems too good to be true, like I am dreaming and will soon find it all a mistake. But here is your letter stating plainly that your business is sold and you will be packed by the time you get an answer. This has been the longest deferred happiness of my life and many times I have feared that I would not be here when you came. At the beginning of each year, though, I have hoped that you would come back to me before its close; then, instead of feeling the disappointment, I have hoped anew for another year.

Such changes as you will find, Father! Changes in the country and changes in me!

Our Territory has become a State, our wilderness has

become a home, and the Snake River Valley gives promise of being one of the richest in the world. Eagle Rock, that was a bleak stage station when Fred's father and I cooked there for the stage company in the early sixties, is a miniature city and calls itself "Idaho Falls." The ladies who throng the social gatherings are wont to doubt me when I boast that one winter I was the only woman who lived there.[26]

The start of cows that you gave me, in the course of twenty years has grown into a herd of several hundred, adding materially to our prosperity.

My own age has more than doubled. You left me a child and will find me past the prime of life and the mother of ten children. Oh, there will be a lot of surprises for you and they will not all be happy ones I fear. You will not be disappointed in Nels, I am sure, for you are broad minded enough to see his goodness in spite of his many petty faults. We have not lived an ideal life, but looking around me, I am forced to admit that he is a better husband and a better father than any I can name. We have experienced prosperity and adversity, sickness and health, hope and despair. We have laid to rest four of our family of ten, but we have met all of it together and unafraid. And looking back over the years, I can truthfully say, "Life has been kind to me." Sometimes I feel that I am the luckiest person in the world for all my wishes have come true. That is, they will have come true when I can welcome you, my father, to the home we have made.

Our home. It is a good substantial, homey home. The rooms are large and the furniture is large to fit them, some of it made by the carpenter according to my orders. We have a new range that seems very big and clumsy to me, more fit for hotel use, but it is a wonder from a cook's point of view, so I think I will learn to like it. We also have water piped into the kitchen. Think of the luxury of it! Your "Em" who used to draw water with an old well sweep to do washing for the aristocratic Southerners, has now but to turn a tap and the water is there.

We keep help in the house all the time now. A girl who is my helper and my companion as well. I have made many young friends in this way and we both have benefitted. Just now we have a wonderfully good girl, Crillia Carson, who is a niece of a girl that Nels wanted to marry before he met me. She declined. However, but he has told me so much about her that it is nice to be in touch with them again. Nels has always been good to get help for me when our means would permit, and his mother, who is with us now, says: "He babies Emma too much." Perhaps it is true, but I feel that I have done my share of the world's work and if I can teach others a few of the things I have learned I can consider myself through.

Yes since I wrote last, Grandfather Just died, just peacefully passed away, and true to her word, the old lady came to us just as soon as he was gone. She is a queer little body, but full of good humor and helpfulness. Insists upon doing for herself in every way and then knits, knits, knits for everyone for pastime.

Now, about the family you are soon to meet. Fred my first born, is a man and my fears that he might follow his father's footsteps were groundless. He has led a rough life, working away from home most of the time since he was twelve, but there have been happy homecomings for the other children are especially fond of their big, cowboy brother.

Jim is his father's helper. Has been doing a man's work since he was fourteen and very often, the work of two or three.

Will is still the peace-maker, so full of wit and originality.

His supply of good humor often turns a bad situation into a laugh. I don't think we have any favorites, for each in his own way is best, but Will is certainly a great joy to us. Francis and Charlie are still just boys. Dutiful, loving lads that will soon be taking their places in the world as their brothers have done.

Then there is the last and least, baby Agnes. Least in size if not least in importance. Of all my babies, she is the only one that you are to see while the least semblance of babyhood is still with her. You asked what you were to bring her from over the seas. I left it up to her and her decision was prompt: "A *boy doll.*"

Now, a long good-bye. Good-bye to pen, ink and paper. I shall be counting the hours until that "White Star Liner" brings you safely back to our own good U. S. A. and to me.

In loving anticipation,
Emma

Epilogue

After the death of Emma's mother on the return trip to England, George Thompson remarried, lost his second wife by death, and then shortly before returning to America in 1891, married Katie Morrell. They resided for a time near the present Firth and Basalt, Idaho vicinity, but Kate was in frail health and pregnant. Both she and their premature baby died, days apart, in November 1892. George Thompson then lived at the Just Ranch until June, 1894, when, visiting his sister Jane Higham "in the poplar country," near Ririe, they both were killed while on a buggy ride, thrown against the abutments of a bridge by a run-away horse. The family has a postcard which George Thompson mailed to Emma on the day he was killed, June 4, 1894. It was delivered several days after his death.

Nels Just continued his ranching activities, as well as interests in mining, banking and civic affairs until March, 1912 when he died of pneumonia in a Salt Lake City hospital. Emma Just continued living in the old home, where she died November 8, 1923. Her death came while the original printing of *Letters of Long Ago* was on the press.

Of her ten children, only her two oldest sons and daughter Agnes survived her.

Emma's oldest son, Fred Bennett, cowboy and rancher, died at his home on the Blackfoot River in 1924. James Just died in 1955. Preceding Nels and Emma in death were George William, who died in 1894 at age 19 while still living at home; Charles who died in 1905; and Francis who died in 1923.

Many of the Just's descendants--now into a seventh generation--still farm or reside on the old property in the Blackfoot River Valley.

Nels and Emma were avid readers, though they had little formal schooling. They endowed their daughter with a thirst for knowledge and a desire to write. When Agnes was 15, in 1901, she went to Albion State Normal College in Albion, Idaho. It was difficult to reach by stagecoach, but it was an Idaho school, and it was her wish to be educated in her home state. After two and a half years there, she attended the Academy at Pocatello, Idaho for about six months. She thought the teachers at Albion were "perfect. They told me to read Emerson and Thoreau, and I'm still reading them," she said in her 1972 interview in preparation for the University of Utah Press publication of the third edition of *Letters of Long Ago*.

Agnes Just's one teaching assignment was for an abbreviated term at the Cedar Creek School, several miles up the Blackfoot River and into the mountains east of the Just Ranch. She had met Robert E. Reid the day after she left Albion Normal. Although he was four years older than the teacher, he was one of the students at the Cedar Creek School in 1905.

Teacher and pupil were married November 28, 1906 in Blackfoot, Idaho. Robert Reid was a son of James and Isabell Goodenough Reid, born in Marsh Valley, Idaho, south of Pocatello, in March, 1884. After their marriage, Robert E. and Agnes Just Reid bought the original homestead property where they reared their sons, Eldro Just, Robert Vincent, Fred Bennett, Douglass J. and Wallace R. Reid. Robert E. Reid died September 21, 1947. After 29 years as his widow, Agnes Just Reid passed on August 7, 1976, one month before her 90th birthday. Their oldest son, Eldro, operated a farm near the Snake River west of Firth until his death in 1993. The other sons still own the old holdings along the Blackfoot River, and along with their children, continue to farm and ranch in the valley.

The Generations

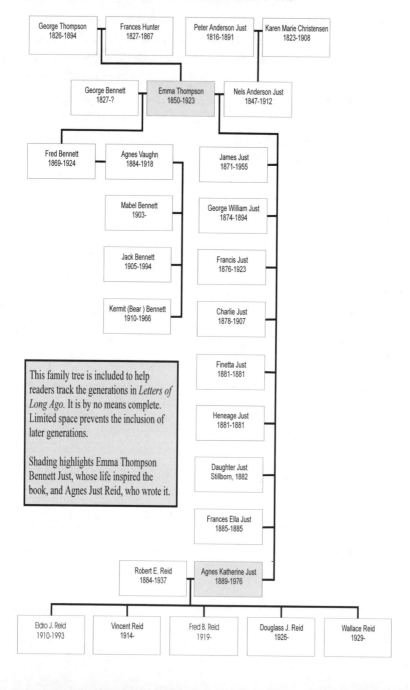

George Thompson
1826-1894

Frances Hunter
1827-1867

Peter Anderson Just
1816-1891

Karen Marie Christensen
1823-1908

George Bennett
1827-?

Emma Thompson
1850-1923

Nels Anderson Just
1847-1912

Fred Bennett
1869-1924

Agnes Vaughn
1884-1918

James Just
1871-1955

Mabel Bennett
1903-

George William Just
1874-1894

Jack Bennett
1905-1994

Francis Just
1876-1923

Kermit (Bear) Bennett
1910-1966

Charlie Just
1878-1907

Finetta Just
1881-1881

This family tree is included to help readers track the generations in *Letters of Long Ago.* It is by no means complete. Limited space prevents the inclusion of later generations.

Shading highlights Emma Thompson Bennett Just, whose life inspired the book, and Agnes Just Reid, who wrote it.

Heneage Just
1881-1881

Daughter Just
Stillborn, 1882

Frances Ella Just
1885-1885

Robert E. Reid
1884-1937

Agnes Katherine Just
1889-1976

Eldro J. Reid
1910-1993

Vincent Reid
1914-

Fred B. Reid
1919-

Douglass J. Reid
1926-

Wallace Reid
1929-

Endnotes

1. The distance from the Blackfoot River site to Malad, county
seat of Oneida County, was about 88 miles which meant that the
ox team made about 11 miles a day. The county records at Malad
contain the following citation of the wedding ceremony of Nels
and Emma: "Nils *[sic]* Anderson Just to Emma Thompson On
the 9th day of November in the year 1870 I solemnised *[sic]* the
Marriage of Nils Anderson Just with Emma Thompson in the
presence of Wm Richards and Frank Carpenter Witnesses J
William Morgan JP Recorded at request of J. W. Morgan
November 18th AD 1870 at [?] oclock PM B. F. White Co Recorder"
Idaho, Oneida County, Clerk, Marriage Book A, page 9.

2. With the discovery of gold on Grasshopper Greek at
Bannock City in 1862 and subsequent discoveries at Virginia
City and Helena, freight wagons and stagecoaches began to travel
the road from Salt Lake City and later Corrine, Utah, to western
Montana. Second in importance only to the Missouri River route,
the Montana Road provided the means of getting thousands of
tons of freight and supplies and many passengers from Utah
and the Central Pacific Railroad to the mining camps of Montana.
The present highway, No. 191-91-Interstate 15 follows rather
closely the old Montana Road which was the principal
thoroughfare for wagon traffic to the north until completion of
the Utah and Northern Railroad in 1884.

3. Old Fort Hall was located on the bottom lands along the Snake River and was off the main stage line to Montana. United States government officials decided to locate a new military post at a point on Lincoln Creek about nine miles southeast of the town of Blackfoot and 40 miles northeast of Old Fort Hall. The new fort was built in May 1870 under the direction of Captain Isaac Putnam.

4. The *New York Sun* was started in 1833 and apparently by the 1870s was receiving rather wide distribution in the West. *Peterson's Magazine* was managed for a long time by Charles Jacob Peterson (1819-1887) and was known variously as the *Ladies National Magazine, Peterson's Ladies National Magazine,* but usually merely *as Peterson's Magazine.* It started in 1843 and Continued until 1898 carrying articles on ladies and children's fashions, cooking recipes, stories, poetry, and other items which might appeal to women readers. Frances Hodgson was evidently one of the many contributors.

5. This was undoubtedly Corbett's Station on the Gilmer & Salisbury Company's stage route to Montana. The station was located about ten miles north of New Fort Hall and, in 1871, also served as the Fort Hall Post Office.

6. In 1865 a Missouri freighter named James Madison (Matt) Taylor built the first bridge across Snake River at Eagle Rock. The toll bridge was eventually acquired by Robert and J. C. Anderson who opened a store, a livery stable, a restaurant, and a bank here. The name, Eagle Rock, was changed to Idaho Falls in 1891.

7. The United States Congress, on March 3, 1871, approved an act establishing an official exploration of the sources of the Missouri and Yellowstone rivers including the area now comprising Yellowstone National Park. Dr. Ferdinand V. Hayden, a nationally recognized geologist, was appointed chief officer of the expedition. In addition a second group under Captains J. W. Barlow and D. P. Heap of the Army Engineer Corps was to make a reconnaissance of the upper Yellowstone, and both parties were to have the protection of a military escort which included Lieutenant Gustavus C. Doane. The Hayden expedition included William H. Jackson as photographer; Thomas Moran, a famous

artist from Philadelphia; and his brother John Moran, a writer. The three groups traveled together and left Ogden, Utah, on June 11, 1871, for the north. They reached Fort Hall near the end of June and then spent a few days camped on the Blackfoot River near Dick Higham's ranch. Frank H. Bradley, a member of the expedition, recorded that the leaders named the nearby mountain next to Blackfoot Valley, Higham's Peak after Emma Just's uncle. It was during this period that Thomas and John Moran visited Mrs. Just.

The date of this letter should be 1871 instead of 1872. Dr. Hayden did lead another expedition in exploration of the Yellowstone Park area and the Teton Range during 1872. William H. Jackson also accompanied this party, taking a number of photographs of the Indians and scenes at the Fort Hall Reservation, but the Moran brothers were not members of this expedition.

The photographs of William H. Jackson and the paintings by Thomas Moran aided Dr. Hayden and others in persuading Congress to enact legislation establishing Yellowstone National Park. The bill was signed into law on March 1, 1872, by President Ulysses S. Grant.

8. Corinne, Utah, was the last construction camp established on the Union Pacific Railroad, and the first Gentile town located in Utah Territory. On March 15, 1869, the *Salt Lake Reporter* announced the selection of the site for Corinne which placed it at the northernmost point on the railroad and at the point where Bear River flows into Great Salt Lake. The town became the freight depot for the transshipment of supplies from the railroad to the mines of eastern Idaho and western Montana.

With the advance of the Utah and Northern Railroad from Franklin, Idaho, to Blackfoot, Idaho, in 1878, Corinne was effectively cut off as a shipping point and rapidly declined, becoming just another small farming community dominated by Mormon families.

9. The Shoemakers lived about two miles down the valley and were for a long time the nearest family in the vicinity.

10. In the summer of 1868, the Bannock and Shoshoni Indians of the Fort Hall area had signed the Treaty of Fort Bridger which assigned them a reservation at Fort Hall. The agency was opened

on April 13, 1869, and various agents then undertook the task of subsisting the Indians while they learned to farm so that they could be relieved of the necessity of their annual nomadic wanderings in search of food. The United States government did not meet its treaty obligations in furnishing food supplies and by April of 1876, almost a thousand Bannock and Shoshoni were starving.

It was finally arranged for them to meet with Idaho Governor D. P. Thompson in July 1876 to whom they expressed their grievances. In addition to the problem of no supplies, a rumor was abroad that the government meant to move all the Indians to Oklahoma Territory. The governor promised to lay their grievances before the authorities in Washington, D.C., but 450 of the Bannock refused to rely on the promises of the Indian Department and traveled to the Plains area during the winter of 1876 to attempt to subsist themselves. See Brigham D. Madsen, *The Bannock of Idaho* (Caldwell, Idaho: The Caxton Printers, Ltd., 1958).

11. In June 1877, the Nez Perce went to war when they refused to give up their Wallowa Valley and move to the Lapwai Reservation. By late August, a Nez Perce raiding party was at Birch Creek, Idaho, on the wagon road to Salmon City. The warriors attacked a wagon train composed of eight freight wagons, thirty mules, and eight drivers and passengers. The Indians killed the three drivers—James Hayden, Tyler Green, and D. Holmes—and two of the passengers, burned the wagons, and drove the mules toward Montana. The Albert Lyon mentioned had been engaged in freighting to the Idaho and Montana mines for several years.

12. The Bannock and Shoshoni at Fort Hall were excited by the Nez Perce War, and it was necessary for the military to warn Agent W. H. Danilson on September 8, 1877, that the Fort Hall Indians were intimidating settlers along the Montana Road by firing guns near the ranches and demanding food. The Just homestead was directly across the Blackfoot River from the Indian reservation and very isolated from any white settlement.

13. At the height of the hysteria caused by the Nez Perce War, a Bannock Indian shot and seriously wounded Robert Boyd and Orson James, two white teamsters who were traveling on

the freight road near the Fort Hall Agency. When the guilty Bannock was arrested on November 23, 1877, a number of Indians gathered around the trading post where a friend of the prisoner, Tambiago, shot and killed Alexander Rhoden, a white man employed as a cattle driver for the agency. The excitement of the Nez Perce War had a definite effect in helping to arouse the Bannock who went to war the following summer, 1878.

14. During the period from 1862 to 1878 while wagon freighters were using the Montana Road, many of them wintered their oxen along the bottom lands of Snake River near Old Fort Hall, a sheltered area which the Indians had used for many years as a place of winter pasturage for their horses. The government agents at the Fort Hall Reservation continually complained of freighters pasturing their stock on reservation lands without paying any compensation to the Bannock and Shoshoni.

15. John W. Young, son of Brigham Young, with the backing of Joseph and Benjamin Richardson of New York City, undertook the building of the Utah Northern Railroad to connect Ogden and Salt Lake City with the northern Utah settlements. Construction began at Brigham City on August 26, 1871, and by the summer of 1874 the road had reached Franklin, Idaho. The Panic of 1873 soon dried up funds for any expansion beyond this point until Jay Gould and other officials of the Union Pacific Railroad took over the little narrow-gauge line on April 3, 1878.

With financing assured, the new company now began to push the renamed Utah and Northern Railroad toward Montana where profits awaited the promoters. By late December 1878 the tracks had been laid beyond the Blackfoot River, and the little town of Blackfoot became the terminus of the line. The road reached Monida Pass on May 9, 1880; Butte, Montana, on December 21, 1881, and a connection with the Northern Pacific at Garrison, Montana, in the fall of 1884. For further details see Merrill D. Beal, *Intermountain Railroads, Standard and Narrow Gauge* (Caldwell, Idaho: The Caxton Printers, 1962).

16. The best accounts of the trial of General Robert T. Burton are those reported by the Salt Lake City newspapers—*Salt Lake Tribune, Daily Herald,* and *Deseret News.* Mark H. Forscutt, "Sketch of Joseph Morris," gives details of the attack on Fort Kington and the killings which resulted, details which were

unknown until a few months ago when the L.D.S. Church Historical Department made the manuscript available to scholars and allowed a copy to be made for the University of Utah Library. Forscutt was clerk of "The First Council of the Church" of the Morrisites, and his fifty-four page manuscript was purchased from him by the L.D.S. Church on June 11, 1903.

On June 13, 1862, Forscutt recorded in his account, the Morrisite people first noticed an approaching armed posse on the bluff south of the Fort. The prophet, Joseph Morris, thereupon retired to his quarters to receive a "revelation" which, when announced to the people, outlined that the posse would attempt to destroy the "saints" but would be unsuccessful—"None of the faithful should be destroyed." Writing long after the event, Forscutt said that some of those who lived through the event had their faith destroyed by "cannon balls and musketry" while the balance "now write 'the prophet' in quotation marks" and came to regard the mission of Morris as "spiritual."

The posse under Robert T. Burton first took action by sending the Morrisite herd boy to deliver the following proclamation to the Morrisite leaders. Forscutt, as clerk of the council, read it:

"Headquarters, Marshal's Posse, Weber River, June 13th, 1862. To Joseph Morris, John Banks, Richard Cook, John Parsons, and Peter Klemgard:

"Whereas, you have heretofore disregarded and defied the judicial officers and laws of the Territory of Utah and whereas, certain writs have been issued for you from the Third Judicial District Court of said Territory, and a sufficient force furnished by the Executive of the same to enforce the laws, this is therefore to notify you *to peaceably* and *quietly* surrender yourselves and the prisoners in your custody forthwith.

"An answer is required in thirty minutes after the receipt of this document if not, forcible measures will be taken for your arrest. Should you disregard this proposition and place your lives in jeopardy, you are hereby required to remove *your women and children;* and all persons *peaceably disposed* are hereby notified to forthwith leave your encampment and are informed that they can find protection with this *posse.*

"H. W. Lawrence, Territorial Marshal, per R. T. Burton and Theodore McKean, Deputies."

After hearing the proclamation, the council leaders gathered the people in the bowery, read the Morris revelation to them, and then Richard Cook started to present the demands of the posse ". . . but before he had time to present it and obtain the decision of the people, the boom of a cannon was heard and almost simultaneously, terrific and heart-rending screams from a young girl who sat on the third seat from the speakers stand. For the moment it was thought to be from fear, but looking on her, the fearful sight of two dead women by her side, and of her lower jaw hanging only by a narrow strip of skin proclaimed the fact, and the barbarity of the horde whose first salutation was a well aimed cannon ball into an assembly of worshipers." The Forscutt manuscript ends at this point.

The testimony of Emma Thompson Just, as reported in the Salt Lake City newspapers, continues the story. The Morrisites resisted the attack by the posse, and fighting went on for two days. On the third day, Sunday afternoon, a white flag was hoisted in the square in front of the school house, and the posse entered the Fort. All the remaining Morrisites, about seventy-five in number, gathered here and watched two horsemen ride out from the group—Burton and another leader of the posse, Joseph L. Stoddard.

Joseph Morris started to speak to his people when one of the men on horseback said that that was enough and commenced firing at Morris. Mrs. Just testified: "I looked at the prophet because I thought no one could kill him. He staggered and fell, and a woman stepped up to Burton and called him a bloodthirsty wretch, and he said no woman should call him that and live, and he shot her. [This was Mrs. James Bowman.] A Mrs. Swanee was also killed .... The same man shot Mrs. Bowman that killed Morris .... We had the impression that none of the faithful could be killed. I didn't think Morris was killed. It seemed to me that he was shot three or four times before he fell, and seeing the wadding I thought the bullets were coming back again. We thought he was like Jesus and would rise again."

George Thompson, father of Emma, then sat on the body of Joseph Morris and exclaimed "You've killed this man, now kill me; I've nothing more to live for." George Richardson, a member of the posse stepped up, leveled his gun at Thompson, and pulled the trigger, but the weapon misfired. Other members of the posse now dragged Thompson away and Burton and Stoddard seized twelve-year-old Emma and attempted to drag her over to the white flag. She seized hold of a cottonwood tree and hung on so desperately that the two men released her.

Emma's testimony ended here. Under cross-examination the

defense attorney made much of the fact that Mrs. Just confused the color of the horse which Burton was riding and also that she and Mrs. Mary Anderson (the girl whose lower jaw was shot away) "were children at the time and their judgment is not to be implicitly trusted." Although Mrs. Just swore under oath that one of the two men on horseback had killed Morris, Mrs. Bowman, and probably Mrs. Swanee, the jury (composed of both Mormons and Gentiles) acquitted Burton partly because Mrs. Just could not positively identify him as the man who did the shooting, being confused about which man was Burton and which one was Stoddard, the latter having been dead for several years. See M. Hamlin Cannon, "The Morrisite War, *American West,* Vol. VII (November 1910), pp. 4-9, 62; *Deseret News* (Salt Lake City), February 17, March 6, 1879, *Salt Lake Daily Herald,* February 17. March 6. 1879; and *Salt Lake Tribune,* February 17, March 6, 1879.

17. Presto Burrell was appointed one of three commissioners of Oneida County when it was created on January 22, 1864. He later moved from Soda Springs and finally settled on a ranch on the Blackfoot River. By the early 1870s, he, Nels Just, Dick Higham, Fred Stevens, and Joe Warren all had ranches on the Blackfoot River, some having settled there as early as 1866.

18. This was probably William Jones, a dissident member of the Morrisites, who, in 1862, had tried to leave Fort Kington but was imprisoned and bound in log chains, along with two others, by the Morrisite leaders. It was the refusal of Joseph Morris and his colleagues to release the three men which led to the issuance of a writ subsequently served with force by a posse under Robert T. Burton.

19. Conant Creek rises in the Teton Mountains in Wyoming and flows westward to form one of the tributaries of Fall River which, in turn, flows into the Snake River.

20. In early 1879, except for a few families at Eagle Rock and some scattered settlers north on Henrys Fork of Snake River, the country was still a wilderness, even the Indians avoided the valley where there were "nine months winter and three months late fall." Several homesteaders built homes on Henrys Fork in the autumn of 1879, but no large-scale settlement occurred until

the Utah and Northern Railroad provided easy travel and communication.

A Mormon, John Poole, first interested the Utah Mormons in the possibilities of the Upper Snake River Valley. He met with L.D.S. church leaders in March 1880, and as a result, a few families began to establish homes in the area from Blackfoot north to what is now St. Anthony, Idaho. But the great migration of Mormon people did not occur until early 1883 when Thomas E. Ricks was named to head the colonization and founded Rexburg on March 11 of that year. By January 1884 there were 815 Mormons in the Upper Snake River Valley and 1,420 residents by the end of the year.

21. The "Irish peddler" was Don Maguire of Ogden, Utah. He not only peddled but became involved in various mining ventures. The Utah State Historical Society has his 169-page diary for the years November 9, 1876, to August 18, 1878. It records his travels and experiences in Utah, Idaho, Montana, and Arizona. Mrs. Reid remembers riding on her first rocking horse in the home of the Maguires in Ogden.

22. The winter of 1886-87 was one of the coldest in the history of the West. In November, snow covered the Rocky Mountains and plains, and after a short respite of a warm "chinook" wind in early January, the worst blizzard in the memory of Western ranchers struck late in the month. Cattle by the thousands died on the plains, the mercury dipped to sixty-eight degrees below zero, and the families on the Blackfoot River were no doubt thankful for their sheltered valley.

23. In 1871 Nels Just started his first ditch with a shovel as a means of excavation. It required 19 years effort to bring his alfalfa field under proper irrigation. The first large canal to be built in the Upper Snake River Valley was the Stewart Canal, taken from Teton River near Teton, Idaho, in June, 1879. Twenty-eight canals were started in the valley between 1881 and 1885, including the Kennedy, Harrison, Coy, Long Island, Egin, Rexburg, Eagle Rock, and Willow Creek. Many others were built during the next three decades until presently there are 120 canals coming out of the upper Snake River.

24. Emma Just served for 14 years as postmistress at the

Presto, Idaho, post office which was named for Presto Burrell.

25. NelsA. Just received a homestead patent on 139.95 acres in Sections 10-11, T2SR37E, March 21, 1889. Then Emma Just bought 160 acres in Section 9, June 8 1889, under the Land Act of April 24, 1820. Next, NelsA. Just patented 143.42 acres under the Timber Culture Act, May 21, 1890. Citations for these transactions are U. S. Bureau of Land Management State Office, General Land Office Patents, Final Certificate Numbers, MT Plat, T2S, R37E, Status of Public Domain Land and Mineral Titles and Acquired Lands (Boise, Idaho).

26. Idaho achieved statehood on July 3, 1890. In 1870 Oneida County extended from the Utah line to Montana and had a population of 1,922 people. The 1880 census reported 6,964 people in Oneida County. Five years later, in 1885, Bingham County was taken away and reported a population of 13,575 in the 1890 census, while the area left in Oneida County showed only 6,819 residents.

Index

A

Albion State Normal College 102

B

Baker, Captain ____: involved in capture of John Wilkes Booth 78
Bear: killed at ranch 53
Bennett, Fred 8, 19, 21; called Nels "Nee" when he was little 3; died 102; Emma sends him away 73; faithful helper during twins' short life 65; first swear word 76; helps with laundry, baby 28; notable penmenship 60; successful fisherman 45; taught to read 31; working away from home 76
Bennett, George: Emma's love for 21
Blackfoot , Idaho: location of 47
Blackfoot River 2, 105, 107
Booth, John Wilkes 78
Bowman, Mrs. James: murdered during Morrisite War 50
Burrell, Presto: difficulty over "lines and cattle" with Nels 59; married 59; post office named after, Nels still at odds with 92
Burton, Robert T.: Emma's testimony freed 51; trial of 48

C

Cabin, Nels and Emma's home 10
Carson, Crillia: neice of girl Nels once wanted to marry, worked for Emma 98
Cattle: the Just herd numbered several hundred at one time 97
Cattle kings: Emma notes the passing of their era 94
Cedar Creek School 102
Chief Joseph 34
Corinne, Utah 25; Nels hauls tallow there 46

D

Dugout: Nels and Emma's first house 6

E

Eagle Rock 15, 25; becomes Idaho Falls 97; circus comes to town 70; Nels brings water to 11

F

Firth 103
Fort Hall 6, 17, 25, 39, 106; Emma baked bread for crew building fort 6; Nels puts up hay there 35; Nels sold beef to soldiers 46

G

Garret, Heneage 25, 28
Gary, Frank: miner who worked for Nels and taught Just children 69

H

Higham, Jane: sister of George Thompson 101
Higham's Peak 107
Hodgson, Frances 7

I

Idaho: statehood 96
Idaho Canal Company 89
Irrigation: Nels' first contract 11, in charge of contract work on Idaho Canal 90

J

Jackson, William H. 107
Jones, William: friend of Just family 61
Judges, Arthur: arrives at Just ranch 52; teaches just children 57; worked for Stevens family 71
Judges, Lewis: arrives at Just ranch 52; tries cowboying, moves to Salt Lake 57; worked for Z.C.M.I. 71
Just, Charles: burned 56; died 102; named by brother 45